"With the experience and insight of an astute clinician, Dr. Swenson offers an abundance of thoughtful, constructive steps to overcome the pressures of contemporary life that impair our efforts to attain balance and find inner peace. *Margin* provides valuable suggestions to every reader interested in physical and emotional health."

—ARMAND NICHOLI, JR., M.D.

"That Dick Swenson has continued to educate readers on the guiding principles of his life and Christian ministry is both needed and exciting. This book remains a great inspiration and practical help to all who read it."

—JAY KESLER

"To a world that demands 'Be all that you can be,' Dr. Richard Swenson brings the sorely needed message that less can be more. Less frenzy, less debt, less obligation—all are ingredients in the abundant life Christ came to give. Loaded with practical suggestions, *Margin* teaches believers to honor God by accepting the limits that are part of His wise creation. Few books can honestly be said to be life-changing—but this is such a book."

—DOUG TROUTEN

"Dr. Swenson is the most insightful diagnostician I know on the world wide epidemic of overload. More importantly, he knows the cure! His prescriptions in *Margin* will rebalance your life, restore your relationships, and renew your joy. I recommend this resource for everyone over age four living in America today."

—DAVID L. STEVENS, M.D.

"Provocative and profound! Dr. Swenson's wisdom and warnings about restoring balance and stewarding time is both sobering and stimulating. This is a keeper."

—JOHN PEARSON, president/CEO, Christian Management Association, San Clemente, California

MARGIN

Restoring Emotional, Physical, Financial,

and Time Reserves to Overloaded Lives

MARGIN

Restoring Emotional, Physical, Financial,

and Time Reserves to Overloaded Lives

RICHARD A. SWENSON, M.D.

NAVPRESS®

BRINGING TRUTH TO LIFE

OUR GUARANTEE TO YOU

We believe so strongly in the message of our books that we are making this quality guarantee to you. If for any reason you are disappointed with the content of this book, return the title page to us with your name and address and we will refund to you the list price of the book. To help us serve you better, please briefly describe why you were disappointed. Mail your refund request to: NavPress, P.O. Box 35002, Colorado Springs, CO 80935.

The Navigators is an international Christian organization. Our mission is to reach, disciple, and equip people to know Christ and to make Him known through successive generations. We envision multitudes of diverse people in the United States and every other nation who have a passionate love for Christ, live a lifestyle of sharing Christ's love, and multiply spiritual laborers among those without Christ.

NavPress is the publishing ministry of The Navigators. NavPress publications help believers learn biblical truth and apply what they learn to their lives and ministries. Our mission is to stimulate spiritual formation among our readers.

© 2004 by Richard A. Swenson

ISBN 1-57683-682-7

Cover design by Charles Brock of UDG DesignWorks, Inc.
Cover photo by Corbis
Creative Team: Don Simpson, Darla Hightower, Arvid Wallen, Pat Miller

Some of the anecdotal illustrations in this book are true to life and are included with the permission of the persons involved. All other illustrations are composites of real situations, and any resemblance to people living or dead is coincidental.

Unless otherwise identified, all Scripture quotations in this publication are taken from the HOLY BIBLE: NEW INTERNATIONAL VERSION® (NIV®). Copyright © 1973, 1978, 1984 by International Bible Society. Used by permission of Zondervan Publishing House. All rights reserved. Other versions used include: the *New American Standard Bible* (NASB), © The Lockman Foundation 1960, 1962, 1963, 1968, 1971, 1972, 1973, 1975, 1977, 1995; *The New Testament in Modern English* (PH), J. B. Phillips Translator, © J. B. Phillips 1958, 1960, 1972, used by permission of Macmillan Publishing Company; and the *King James Version* (KJV).

Swenson, Richard A.
  Margin : restoring emotional, physical, financial, and time reserves to overloaded lives / Richard A. Swenson.--Rev. ed.
    p. cm.
  Includes bibliographical references and index.
  ISBN 1-57683-682-7
  1. Christian life. 2. Stress (Psychology)--Religious aspects--Christianity. 3. Time management--Religious aspects--Christianity. 4. Success--Religious aspects--Christianity. I. Title.
  BV4501.3.S945 2004
  155.9'042--dc22

                            2004009175

Printed in the United States of America

3 4 5 6 7 8 9 10 /10 09 08 07 06

FOR A FREE CATALOG OF NAVPRESS BOOKS & BIBLE STUDIES,
CALL 1-800-366-7788 (USA) OR 1-800-839-4769 (CANADA)

For Linda

It's hard to imagine this book—or life—

without your presence and love.

CONTENTS

ACKNOWLEDGMENTS

THIS BOOK WAS ten years in the making, which means that a number of deserving people waited a long time for their official acknowledgment.

Bill Tomfohr, perhaps more than any other, kept the work alive in the early years. For preliminary ideas about the theme of margin, credit goes to Ralph Suechting. I wish to thank those who read portions of the book during the formative process for their comments and criticisms: Bill Thedinga, Walter Schultz, Dan Johnson, Hector Cruz, Mike Simpson, and Jim Eggert.

Many contributed in various other ways, including: Ted and Jae Anderson, Everett and Genevieve Wilson, Ruth Swenson, Caroline Miller, Jerry and Marcie Borgie, Craig and Linda Wilson, Aggie Wagner, Donna Knipfer, Chuck and Becky Folkestad, Dave and Judy Hatch, Hazel Bent, Betty Cruz, Gail Thedinga, Mary Schultz, and Michael Bailey. In addition, I remain grateful to family and friends around the world who have demonstrated their sustained and prayerful interest in this project.

I owe a great debt of gratitude to Don Simpson, whose counsel was always as accurate as it was gracious. As editor, Steve Webb was both an enthusiastic supporter of the author and a faithful advocate for the reader. Knollwood Lodge was initially timely and later essential for allowing special arrangements to write in that beautiful, secluded winter retreat.

My wife, Linda, has been encourager and critic, copy editor and typist, reader and researcher—in short, collaborator throughout the entire decade. This work would have been abandoned long ago without her help. Our two sons, Matt and Adam, (and now daughter-in-law, Maureen) have been more than patient, but are nevertheless pleased at the prospect of having their parents returned to them.

My margin has been devoted to writing for a very long time. It will be an uncommon joy to devote it once again to my family.

MARGINLESS LIVING

THE CONDITIONS OF modern-day living devour margin. If you are homeless, we send you to a shelter. If you are penniless, we offer you food stamps. If you are breathless, we connect you to oxygen. But if you are marginless, we give you yet one more thing to do.

Marginless is being thirty minutes late to the doctor's office because you were twenty minutes late getting out of the bank because you were ten minutes late dropping the kids off at school because the car ran out of gas two blocks from the gas station—and you forgot your wallet.

Margin, on the other hand, is having breath left at the top of the staircase, money left at the end of the month, and sanity left at the end of adolescence.

Marginless is the baby crying and the phone ringing at the same time; margin is Grandma taking the baby for the afternoon. Marginless is being asked to carry a load five pounds heavier than you can lift; margin is a friend to carry half the burden. Marginless is not having time to finish the book you're reading on stress; margin is having the time to read it twice.

Marginless is fatigue; margin is energy.

Marginless is red ink; margin is black ink.

Marginless is hurry; margin is calm.

Marginless is anxiety; margin is security.

Marginless is culture; margin is counterculture.

Marginless is the disease of the new millennium; margin is its cure.

Pieces of Broken Humanity

It was my lunch hour on a beautiful autumn day, but I didn't mind. A bloody towel clutched over a bloody face revealed the need.

At seventy-six, John was slim, fit, and active. Following retirement and a heart attack, he determined to take care of himself and have fun at the same time. It was Wisconsin in the summer and Florida in the winter, but mostly it was golf every day.

As his wife was otherwise occupied, John challenged Glen to eighteen holes. Approaching the first hole, John drove his ball down the middle of the fairway and then moved to the side. Glen prepared his ball, lifted the club, and swung vigorously. The ball, however, angled hard to the right and struck John in the eye. Blood instantly came gushing out as his eyeball dropped into his hand.

By the time they arrived at the clinic, Glen was still as white as a sheet. The injured John, however, was obviously enjoying himself—even though covered with blood.

"I guess Glen never knew I had an artificial eye," he twinkled. "I popped it out to make sure it wasn't broken. I didn't really mean to scare him like that."

Rarely a day goes by that I don't pick up some broken pieces of humanity and attempt to put them back together again. In John's case, the wounds turned out to be humorous, and his lacerated eyebrow was easily sutured. Unfortunately, not all patients have stories that are humorous. And not all "broken pieces" are so easily repaired.

Some people come in for broken legs; others, broken hearts. Some have irritable colons; others, irritable spouses. Some have bleeding ulcers; others, bleeding emotions. And compounding these wounds, many patients show signs of a new disease: marginless living.

How often do I see the effects of marginless living? About every fifteen minutes. Into my office on a regular basis comes a steady parade of exhausted, hurting people. The reason these patients come to me, however, is not to discuss their lack of margin. They don't even know what margin is. Instead, they come because of pain. Most don't realize that pain and the absence of margin are related.

The Unexpected Pain of Progress

That our age might be described as painful comes as a discomforting surprise when we consider the many advantages we have over previous generations. Progress has given us unprecedented affluence, education, technology, and entertainment. We have comforts and conveniences other eras could only dream about. Yet somehow, we are not flourishing under the gifts of modernity as one would expect.

Why do so many of us feel like air-traffic controllers out of control? How can the salesman feel so stressed when the car is loaded with extras, the paycheck is bigger than ever, and vacation lasts four weeks a year? How is it possible that the homemaker is still tired despite the help of the washing machine, clothes dryer, dishwasher, and vacuum cleaner? If we are so prosperous, why are the therapists' offices so full? If we have ten times more material abundance than our ancestors, why are we not ten times more content and fulfilled?

Something has gone wrong. If you know what pain wounds look like, you will see them on all your friends. This book is dedicated to exposing and correcting the specific kind of pain that comes from marginless living. Why? Because we find ourselves in the midst of an unnamed epidemic. The disease of marginless living is insidious, widespread, and virulent.

The New Universal Constant

The marginless lifestyle is a relatively new invention and one of progress's most unreasonable ideas. Yet in a very short time it has become a nearly universal malady. Few are immune. It is not limited to a certain socioeconomic group, nor to a certain educational level. Even those with a deep spiritual faith are not spared. Its pain is impartial and nonsectarian—everybody gets to have some.

Do you know families who feel drawn and quartered by overload? Do you know wage earners who are overworked, teachers who are overstressed, farmers who are overextended, pastors who are overburdened, or mothers of young children who are overwhelmed? Chances are the pathogen of marginless living is largely responsible.

One would think that physicians, the acknowledged pain experts, would be exempt. Not so. As a profession, we suffer deeply from the absence of margin. Consequently, I know of the extent and seriousness of this condition from three sources. First, I have observed it in the lives of patients. Second, I saw its effects in the lives of the interns and residents I taught for fifteen years. Third, I know of the weight of marginless living because for a long time it sat on my chest. Decades ago I paid the ransom and purchased back margin, a decision that cost me significant income. Yet it was one of the wisest purchases I've ever made. I have no regrets.

WHY ALL THE FUSS?

Because most of us do not yet know what margin is, we also do not know what marginless is. We feel distressed, but in ill-defined ways. We can tell life isn't quite what it used to be or perhaps not quite what we expected it should be. Then we look at our cars, homes, and big screen TVs and conclude that our distress must be in our imaginations.

Others deny vehemently that anything is wrong. "Life has always been hard," they say. "People have always been stressed. It is simply part of living. There has always been change to cope with. There have always been economic problems, and people have always battled depression. It is the nature of life to have its ups and downs—so why all the fuss?"

I'm not the one who's making the fuss; I'm only writing about it. I'm only being honest about what I see all around me. Something's wrong. People are tired and frazzled. People are anxious and depressed. People don't have the time to heal anymore. There is a psychic instability in our day that prevents peace from implanting itself very firmly in the human spirit. And despite the skeptics, this instability is not the same old nemesis recast in a modern role. What we have here is a brand-new disease.

To be sure, the pains of the past were often horrible beyond description. To have your wife die in childbirth, your children crippled with polio, your cattle ravaged by tuberculosis, and your crops leveled by locusts is not the common definition of the good life. But those were the pains of the past, and most of them are gone. Unfortunately—and unexpectedly—the pains of progress are now here to take their place. Prominent among them is the disease of marginless living.

THE FOCUSING VALUE OF PAIN

No one likes pain. We all want to get rid of it as soon as possible. But physical pains are usually there for a reason, to tell us something is wrong and needs to be fixed. Emotional, relational, and societal pains, too, are often indicators that all is not well. As such, they serve a valuable purpose—they help us focus.

Modern-day living, however, opposes focusing. Surrounded by frenzy and interruptions, we have no time for anything but vertigo. So our pain, it turns out, is actually an ally of sorts. In the hurt is a help. Pain first gets our attention—as it does so well—and then moves us in the opposite direction of the danger.

If you were my patient, you would come to me already focused on your pain. You would want me to explain it and make it go away. My responsibility would be to listen to your symptoms, diagnose your problem, and offer a prescription. And because drawing diagrams often helps us to understand, I might write it on a prescription pad for you to remember. Perhaps it would look something like this:

Rx: *From the Desk of . . .*

Richard A. Swenson, M.D.

SYMPTOM:	PAIN
DIAGNOSIS:	OVERLOAD
PRESCRIPTION:	MARGIN
PROGNOSIS:	HEALTH

IS THERE A CURE?

If we focus and work to understand, is this painful disease of marginless living curable? Is health possible? Of course it is. But the kind of health I speak of will seldom be found in "progress" or "success." For that reason, I'm not sure how many are willing to take the cure. But at least we all deserve a chance to understand the disease.

PART ONE

THE PROBLEM

PAIN

THE PAIN OF PROGRESS

ERICK OSTROM WAS born in Sweden in 1894 and came to the United States at the age of eighteen. No one is quite sure why he came, for Grandpa didn't talk about it. Not knowing the language and having only a third-grade education, he sometimes slept in theaters while going from job to job. Later he married Anna, whose love and gentleness buffered but could not prevent the hardness of life. The Ostroms had six children, losing two of them in infancy—the causes of their deaths unknown. Grandpa would tell of transporting one of the dead infants in a blizzard to the neighboring town, burying her there in the frozen ground.

During the Great Depression, Grandpa developed tuberculosis. He was in and out of the sanitarium for the next eleven years, had one of his lungs removed, and was never again to reach one hundred pounds. The doctors told him he probably contracted the disease in the steel mills. To make ends meet, the children began working while Anna cleaned houses and took in washing. After his release, the family tried farming, but the cows got sick and Grandpa got sicker.

Although he lived to the remarkable age of eighty-four, life was always hard for Grandpa. It never did get easy. Neither did he expect that it would.

If my grandfather could have asked for whatever he wanted to make his life easier during those difficult years, he would have requested health for himself and his family, and that his babies would not die from unnamed diseases. He would have wished for education, a warm home in the winter, and a reliable supply of food. He might have requested a team of horses, good seed, and fertilizer. Perhaps he would have wished to visit his family in Sweden.

All of these advantages have been granted in America today. Yet the formula for happiness has proven to be more elusive than the simple bestowing of these benefits. Somewhere the equation has broken down. Food plus health plus warmth plus education plus affluence have not quite equaled Utopia. We live with unprecedented wealth and all it brings. We have leisure, entertainment, convenience, and comfort. We have insulated ourselves from the unpredictable ravages of nature. Yet stress, frustration, and oftentimes even despair unexpectedly accompany our unrivaled prosperity.

PROGRESS AND PANDEMONIUM

While visiting our family recently, an eleven-year-old friend from a large city announced, "There's an epidemic going on down there. I think it's pandemonium."

We live in a troubled age. For every problem that has a solution, there is a solution that brings another problem. Few know where we are headed, but universally acknowledge that we are careening along at breakneck speed.

How can this be? Aren't we advancing, improving, evolving? Aren't technological development and social learning bringing us an ever better world? Never did we suspect that pandemonium and progress would one day walk on stage together, or that pain and progress would one day join forces against us.

Exactly what is progress? Simply stated, progress means proceeding to a higher stage of development. "The idea of progress," explains historian Robert Nisbet, "holds that mankind has advanced in the past . . . is now advancing, and will continue to advance through the foreseeable future. From at least the early nineteenth century until a few decades ago, belief in the progress of mankind, with Western civilization in the vanguard, was virtually a universal religion on both sides of the Atlantic."[1] Progress was automatic, the inevitable function of chronology, and the flow of progress was assumed to be inherently positive.

Progress is so natural an idea that twenty-first-century Westerners can't conceive of life without it. The modern mind has been so reared under its assumptions that devising alternative scenarios seems impossible. If not progress, then what? Regress? Who in their right mind would advocate regress? Even the connotations of these words are laden with bias. Progression is forward; regression is backward. Enlightenment versus primitivism.

Most of us trust the idea of progress more than we realize. It is the train we all boarded for the ride to the good life. "*We have faith in progress*," observes philosopher Nicholas Wolterstorff. "Until recently, the general public . . . regarded modernization as a good thing, typically giving it the honorific title 'development.' Development was touted as the cure to a multitude of human miseries."[2]

Is there a disease? We will soon have a remedy. Is there poverty? We have enough wealth to go around, and a social program or two will solve the problem of the poor. Is there an energy shortage? We will find new technologies to harness the power of the nucleus and to capture the sun. Is there famine? We will use fertilizers and hybrid seeds to conquer hunger. We grew to assume that the solution to any problem could be confidently entrusted to progress. Thanks to its blessings, we came to perceive the future as a safer place to live.

FAILED FAITH

For a while, it appeared progress was going to lead us to the mountaintop, and we were euphoric in anticipation. One after another, progress paraded before us its spectacular successes, prominent among which were an incredible array of technical achievements that test the limits of imagination. We can now transplant both the heart and lungs and get you out of the hospital in six days. We have robots that work, cars that talk, and trains that hover. From atom smashers to earth movers to "smart" bombs, it is an amazing age.

Then, almost without warning, failures began to take their place on stage alongside the successes—first a few, then more, and now many. As a result, our enthusiasm for both progress and the future has moderated. Polls reveal many Americans are no longer confident their children will have a better life than they did.

It is not my intention to denigrate the value of progress's achievements. We have all benefited greatly. As a physician, I understand the tremendous advantages of immunizations, antibiotics, and anesthesia. We all marvel at the power of communications and the speed of transportation. The print media has vastly increased access to learning. Wealth has permitted opportunities far beyond the imagining of our great-grandparents.

The United States in particular has been a prodigy from the womb of progress. Our technology is celebrated, our medicine awe-inspiring, our universities prestigious, and our research of consistent Nobel-Prize quality. Knowledge of our language is desired the world over. Our freedoms set a standard for other nations to compare themselves to.

Yet as visible as these achievements have been, our faults demand a glaring prominence of their own: debt, divorce, teenage pregnancy, illicit drug abuse, crime, incarceration rates, corporate malfeasance, AIDS, litigation, educational breakdown and functional illiteracy, unaffordable health care . . . If progress is so wonderful, why do we drink and drug to forget our problems? Why are we divorcing and suing at such rates? Why are people killing themselves—and others—in such numbers?

TOO MUCH PAIN

Analyzing progress and social trends from this macroscopic view lends a valuable perspective. But we do not see pain as clearly from this distance as we do when it sits in front of us. Pain comes alive when it talks—even more so when it cries. My initial observations about progress, pain, and margin came not from the distance of the macroscope but instead from the closeness of my examining table. One patient at a time, one story at a time. I worry about the deteriorating statistics, but numbers don't feel pain. It's the face I see behind each statistic that motivates me to write.

These patients are stressed, depressed, and exhausted. Some are desperate. Their jobs are insecure. Their farms have been repossessed. They are over their heads in debt. Their marriages are in trouble. They worry about the cultural forces nipping at the heels of their children.

These patients don't know what to do or where to turn. They have no social supports, no roots, no community. Their stomachs won't stop burning, and they can't sleep at night. For them, the promise of progress has too often soured into personal and relational pain.

THE SABOTAGING OF MARGIN

There can be little doubt that the contemporary absence of margin is linked to the march of progress. In a general sense, those cultures with the most progress are the same as those with the least margin. If you were wondering why there is a chapter on progress in a book on margin, this is the reason. Margin has been stolen away, and progress was the thief. If we want margin back, we will first have to do something about progress.

To help us understand how progress sabotages margin, let's examine how progress functions and the natural consequences of its behavior. The first principle to understand is that because of differentiation, progress ALWAYS gives us MORE.

> **Axiom #1:** Progress works by differentiating our environment, thus always giving us more and more of everything faster and faster.

Let me illustrate how progress differentiates our environment. If progress differentiates a tree, it makes tables, chairs, bowls, and toothpicks. If progress differentiates a piece of cloth it makes hankies, shirts, socks, and hats. If progress differentiates a mountain, it divides the mountain into copper, silver, gold, lead, iron, and tailings. If progress differentiates our time, it splits it into hours, minutes, seconds, and then nanoseconds. If progress differentiates our workplace, it finds ways for work to happen on the road, in the car, at home, in hotels, and in conference centers. If progress differentiates our ministries, it first looks at a continent, then a country, then the people and language groups within that country. The manner in which progress evolves, therefore, ALWAYS results in more and more of everything faster and faster. It is *impossible* for progress to give us less and less slower and slower.

As a consequence of progress differentiating (and then proliferating), it increases everything it touches. This is not necessarily a bad result. To the contrary, it is almost always the desired result. The American definition of happiness is, after all, "more than I have now," and progress provides "more" in abundance. However, there are additional consequences to this "more" that were not initially anticipated. We are ready for the second axiom.

> **Axiom #2:** The spontaneous flow of progress is toward increasing stress, change, complexity, speed, intensity, and overload.

This axiom might seem accusatory against progress, or perhaps biased in favor of a nostalgic past. Or perhaps this statement takes you by surprise, for we are often conditioned to think of progress in terms of benign abundance. But let me assure you, the statement is one of science, of pure and easily provable mathematics. It will be further clarified in chapter 4— The Pain of Stress and chapter 5—The Pain of Overload (see also chapter 2 in my book *The Overload Syndrome*[3]).

That progress flows strongly in the direction of increased pressure on the individual and on the system has come as a rude shock to almost all observers. And when the "more and more of everything faster and faster" of progress collides with the established fact of human limits, margin disappears. These consequences are summarized in the following axioms.

> **Axiom #3:** All humans have physical, mental, emotional, and financial limits that are relatively fixed.

Axiom #4: The profusion of progress is on a collision course with human limits. Once the threshold of these limits is exceeded, overload displaces margin.

Axiom #5: On the unsaturated side of their limits, humans can be open and expansive. On the saturated side of these limits, however, the rules of life totally change.

Please understand: progress is not evil. Similarly stress, change, complexity, speed, intensity, and overload are, for the most part, not enemies. But we have different conditions at play than at any other time in our history, and we must discern our course carefully lest we be overwhelmed by forces out of control.

We must have some room to breathe. We need freedom to think and permission to heal. Our relationships are being starved to death by velocity. No one has the time to listen, let alone love. Our children lay wounded on the ground, run over by our high-speed good intentions. Is God now pro-exhaustion? Doesn't He lead people beside the still waters anymore? Who plundered those wide-open spaces of the past, and how can we get them back? There are no fallow lands for our emotions to lie down and rest in. We miss them more than we suspect.

Certainly one cannot blame all the pains of the world on lack of margin. But it is fair to say that the lack of margin is a much greater component of our pain than most realize.

FAULTY PREMISES

In its specifics, the definition of progress varies from culture to culture and from age to age. Within contemporary American society, however, our notion of progress was first defined and later dominated by money, technology, and education. Each of these areas is of value, but none of them cares much about our transcendent needs. That indifference constitutes a serious failure.

Americans have a widespread perception that inextricably associates our overall well-being with our material and cognitive status. This, in fact, is how we measure progress. If we earn a degree, get a raise, and buy a new house, we are automatically "better-off." But what about the depressed schoolteacher, the recently divorced executive, the suicidal adolescent, or the octogenarian being force-fed in the nursing home? By what economic and cognitive parameters do we measure their "progress"?

In our enthusiasm to improve material and cognitive performance, we neglected to respect other more complex and less objective parameters along the way. The social, emotional, and spiritual contributions to our well-being were, and continue to be, overlooked and underestimated. Not only are they more difficult to measure, but we apparently believed they would simply "improve" along with everything else. Or else, in our rush for the future, we didn't care.

So when the family began to crumble, we didn't know what to think of it. When mobility began to tear apart community, we took little notice. When psychological stress and pain appeared on nearly every doorstep, we attempted to invalidate it. Our paradigm does not know how to accommodate this type of data. If you are better off, then how can you be worse off? Since you have progressed, you cannot feel sick. As long as the stock market is up and houses are bigger, you must be doing well—even if you're not.

Did progress betray us? Not really. We should have known from the start there was more to life than material and cognitive well-being. Until we understand what progress is and isn't (that is, should be and can never be), we will remain trapped in a paradigm that is not taking us where we need to be going.

REGAINING CONTROL

Should we jettison progress and start over? That would not be wise. We do not really wish to abandon its many benefits. But neither do we any longer wish to endure its complications.

Is there perhaps another option available to us? Can we put progress on probation while we work out its problems? Two actions would be required of us for this approach to succeed: First, we must regain control of progress; and second, we must redirect it.

To control progress will not be easy. If we decide to put on the brakes, which pedal do we push? If we want to call "foul," which referee should we approach? To what authority does progress submit? The answer is: None. There are no brakes, no referees, no authorities.

After gaining an autonomous strength, progress has built up a good head of steam; it does not depend on us to push it along. The trouble is, it no longer responds to us either. Progress calls the shots. When it wrestles, it wins. If progress and pain are linked, well, a little pain never hurt anyone. If progress and margin are enemies, well, what is margin? So what if we are all stressed and overloaded? We are addicted, and progress knows it. We now do its bidding. Before we can subjugate progress, we must first break the addiction.

As we subjugate progress, we first make it subservient to our greater goals and needs, especially relationships. We once again practice economics "as if people mattered." We once again agree that things do not own us and are not even very important. We once again assert that jobs are only jobs, that cars are only organized piles of metal, that houses will one day fall down—but that people are important beyond description. We once again assert that love stands supreme above all other forces, even to the ends of the universe and beyond.

A MATTER OF (RE)DIRECTION

I am not abandoning progress, and I am not for regress. But I am for redirection.

If you are traveling from Chicago to New York and instead find yourself in Houston, the sensible thing to do is to stop the car, consult the map, and turn in the right direction. In the same way, if we have traveled down the road of progress and now find ourselves in a situation where stress and overload rule our daily schedules, and where margin as a component of living has disappeared, we do not need to apologize for stopping and redirecting ourselves.

Perhaps we should not go any further until we have accomplished this redirection and defined progress in more wholesome terms. Perhaps we ought to defer the future for a while until we have developed a satisfactorily integrated model to guide our journey. Under the new understanding of accounting we would not call it progress if we gained in wealth but lost in relationship; we would not call it beneficial if we improved in estate but injured the psyche; and we would not call it profitable if we achieved a promotion but lost spiritual integrity.

Until we find ways to guard our mental and spiritual health as well as our social ecology, we will only compound our troubles. Only when progress begins to show discipline and restraint, as well as a respect for the inward and transcendent needs of human beings—including our need for margin—will we again be able to trust it.

RIGHT RELATIONSHIPS

Progress's biggest failure has been its inability to nurture and protect right relationships. If progress had helped here, I would have no quarrel with it. As we have already seen, progress builds by using the tools of economics, education, and technology. But what are the tools of the relational life? Are they not the social (my relationship to others), the emotional (my relationship to myself), and the spiritual (my relationship to God)? None of the tools of progress has helped build the relational foundation our society requires.

Margin, however, knows how to nurture relationship. In fact, margin *exists* for relationship. Progress, on the other hand, has little to say about the relational life. Even our language gives us away. When we talk of progress, we do not mean social, emotional, and spiritual advancement. In analyzing our age, commentator after commentator will demonstrate how much better-off we are. Yet, invariably, they are talking about money, energy, transportation, housing, communications, technology, and education. People, however, have relational needs that go much deeper. And while all the focus was on the material and cognitive, our relational environments suffered from neglect.

FIVE ENVIRONMENTS

MOST OF OUR **PROGRESS**:
1. Physical environment (wealth, technology, health—the material world)
2. Cognitive environment (knowledge, information, education—the intellectual world)

MOST OF OUR **PAIN**:
3. Social environment (family, friends, neighbors, church—the societal world)
4. Emotional environment (feelings, attitudes—the psychological world)
5. Spiritual environment (the eternal and transcendent—God)

While the progress we boast of is found within the material and cognitive environments, most of the pain we suffer is found within the social, emotional, and spiritual. The material and cognitive environments are unquestionably important. They also have an advantage in that they are more visible and thus more highly pursued. Scripture teaches us, however, that the social, emotional, and spiritual environments are even more important.

How might we know that the relational environments are where God would have us concentrate? Simply put, these are the same areas Christ spent His time developing and where His teaching is focused.

Where do you think God would have us search for answers regarding drugs, crime, divorce, suicide, depression, teenage pregnancies, sexually transmitted diseases, and litigation? In the material and cognitive realms, or in the relational ones? Our society tries in vain to remedy these problems using the popular notions of progress—appropriating more money (that is, material/physical answers) and setting up more classes (that is, cognitive/educational answers). But insufficient funds and lack of education are not the problem. The problem is lack of love.

With the establishment of a proper emphasis, all appropriate needs will be met. Should we fail in this task, however, progress will only bring us increasing pain. Our wallets will get fatter, our houses bigger, our cars faster, and our brains smarter. Yet when we neglect the most important priorities, our final reward will fittingly be all the unhappiness money can buy.

MEASURING PROGRESS

Progress—tempting, willful, arrogant, divisive, unruly, godlike—what shall we do with you? We have trusted your guidance and followed your lead. In many ways, you've tried to build a successful world. But you have been getting us into trouble of late. We need to stop doing the things that get us into trouble and start doing better things.

"The whole point," contends British economist E. F. Schumacher, "is to determine what constitutes progress."[4] What should constitute progress? Suspending our "chronological arrogance," let's stay with the British and back up to the days before progress had much momentum. Two centuries ago, an eloquent statesman stood before England and battled tirelessly—and successfully—the evils of slavery. William Wilberforce served in Parliament for forty-five years, universally honored for his integrity.

In his influential writings, Wilberforce makes several references to the importance of progress. Yet it is not progress in wealth, education, and power that he speaks of, but instead, progress in virtue. This, he suggests, could be measured by "the fear and love of God and of Christ; love, kindness, and meekness toward our fellow men; indifference to the possessions and events of this life compared with our concern about eternity; self-denial and humility."[5] It does not sound much like our current definition of progress, but it does sound hopeful.

Discerning Christians have long known that God is not impressed with our wealth, education, or power.[6] Nevertheless, we have labored eagerly in those fields. What if, instead, we were to begin measuring our progress not by our wealth but by our virtue; not by our education but by our humility; and not by our power but by our meekness?

Graduate degrees and GNPs will never usher in the kingdom—only love can do that. And love brings us back to Wilberforce: "Above all, measure your progress by your experience of the love of God and its exercise before men." [7]

THE PAIN OF PROBLEMS

SEVERAL YEARS AGO, I attended a late-night delivery by a very young-looking twenty-two-year-old mother. As I was the faculty member "on call" and simply assisting the resident with the case, I had not met the family before.

This was Brenda's first baby. She was acting bravely despite her discomfort. An occasional cry escaped as the contraction peaked. Then she would close her eyes in exhaustion and await the next wave of pain.

The nurse who both coached and comforted Brenda would occasionally glance over to the window ledge where the husband sat watching television. Brenda had a long second stage of labor, and we were in the room for over two hours. But I never heard him utter a sound.

The resident and nurse were doing most of the work with the patient, so I just stood back and watched. Then I leaned against the wall and watched. I was tired. But despite my tiredness, I was also fascinated by the increasingly bizarre social event that was unfolding.

It was around midnight. Brenda's labor happened to coincide with the end of one slasher-type movie and the beginning of another. The final hour of the first movie was filled with violence: knifings, bloody machine gun fights, exploding cars and boats.

The nurse and I looked at each other and rolled our eyes in disgust. Should we demand the set be turned off? Mercifully, the first movie was wrapping up, body bags all over the place.

By this time, the baby's head was crowning. Brenda was still fairly well controlled, but her cries were getting louder and lasting longer. Another ten minutes, I figured.

Still no response from the husband, who was settling in for the beginning of the next movie. On the television screen, a father and small child were strolling down a city street when they stopped to watch a clown act. Suddenly, one of the clowns grabbed the little boy and took off running. With the boy yelling "Daddy, Daddy!" the clown leaped into the back of a waiting van, the father in pursuit. Just as the vehicle started to pull away, the father tore open the back door. The clown inside shot the father point blank in the face. Blood was everywhere.

Just then—exactly then—Brenda screamed and the baby was born.

Go back inside, little one, I thought. *You really don't know what kind of world awaits you.*

DIFFERENT GAME, DIFFERENT RULES, DIFFERENT STAGE

As this baby will surely grow up to discover, we live in a problem-laden world. If these problems would stay in one place, perhaps we'd have a better chance at solving them. But progress has given them wings. And with the advantage of speed, problems are harder to hit than a swooping bat at midnight.

Not only have problems picked up speed, but so has history itself. The flow of history is now the flood of history. The "throughput" of change, information, and people has accelerated explosively. Despite our best attempts to manage the sweep of events, history has escaped. Now we count ourselves fortunate if we are even able to track it, let alone predict it, interpret it, or manage it.

In the past, progress implied upward and onward, and we developed a linear, ascending way of thinking. Somewhere in the last few decades, however, we took a quantum leap off the straight line. The astounding acceleration of change and the increasing complexity and interrelatedness of issues have time-warped us into a new era.

Despite uninformed claims to the contrary, we live in an unprecedented day with unprecedented problems. We have been disarticulated from our own past and do not yet know how to deal with the present, let alone the future. Having been selected to live out this great drama, we are playing a different game by different rules on a different stage than any other people in the history of the world.

THE GOLDEN FRAME OF NOSTALGIA

That we live in an unprecedented era with unprecedented problems would seem to be self-evident, yet I sometimes have difficulty convincing people of this. Many insist that "there is nothing new under the sun" and especially disdain the whining and sniveling of the weak who complain incessantly about life's problems. When you discuss these difficulties with them, a challenge invariably results: "Life isn't any different now," they say. "Sure, that little newborn baby might have a difficult life—but people have *always* had problems and always will. If you went back to the 'good old days,' you couldn't stand it for a week. You'd come flying back to the 'troubled' twenty-first century in a flash!"

Too often the discussion of contemporary problems ends up being detoured by this same debate about the past. People assume that expressing concerns about today's world implies a preference for yesterday's world. But this is a detour I don't wish to make.

Comparisons with the past are risky. Our tendency is to select what we wish to remember and conveniently forget the rest. "Christians in particular are prone to abbreviate the historical record, pruning from the past that which is messy," explains Notre Dame historian Nathan Hatch. "By a subtle and often unconscious process we pick out of the historical tapestry only those strands which reinforce our own points of view."[1] Or, as Jackie Gleason quipped, "The past remembers better than it lived." So when I say that our age is difficult and our problems are unprecedented, it does not mean I am pining for a romanticized past. It only means that our age is difficult and our problems are unprecedented.

In fairness to the skeptics and stoics, I will concede that comparisons between times present and times past do reveal several similarities:

1. We have problems, and our ancestors had problems.
2. Our problems are painful, and our ancestors' problems were painful.
3. We have some advantages in our lifestyle, and our ancestors had some advantages in their lifestyle.

All of this is true—so far as it goes. But where we differ radically from our ancestors and indeed, even from our own recent past, is that suddenly, almost overnight, an entire new wave of social, technological, and economic experience has descended upon us. It is as if history sneezed, and we have been thrown into a different trajectory.

Figure 3.1—Unprecedented . . .

a partial list

Speed of travel	Speed of communication
Power of computers	Number of scientists/researchers
Information age	Collapse of information float
Litigation levels	Media pervasiveness and power
Technological advances	Energy utilization and dependence
Complexity	Specialization
Shrinking world	Widespread globalization
Tightly coupled world system	Electronic money
National indebtedness	International indebtedness
Corporate indebtedness	Personal indebtedness
Population congestion	Traffic congestion, land and air
Vulnerability to terrorism	Destructive power of weaponry
Mobility	Prevalence of divorce

Overpopulated prisons	Availability of illicit drugs
AIDS	Abortion
Aging populace	Disintegration of extended family
Changing role of women	Daycare for children
Disappearance of traditions	Disappearance of community

Each item listed has played a significant role in making our era different from all those that preceded it. And when we factor in the interrelatedness of issues, the dimensions involved, and the speed of change, then unprecedented becomes too mild a word.

To help us understand it better, let's explore how the claim "unprecedented" is both a statement of history and, importantly, a statement of mathematics.

LESSONS OF HISTORY

History is a valuable teacher. Yet when I maintain that we live in an unprecedented era, it implies that the lessons of history will only be marginally successful in framing our questions and suggesting our remedies. Having navigated ourselves off the map, we do not know what is around the next bend. Furthermore, we cannot depend on the lessons of history to tell us, for history, too, has never been here before.

I am certainly not intending to deprecate the tremendous value of a historical perspective. I am aware that to disqualify history, even partially, is at best presumptuous and at worst idiotic. We should all be warned, however, that at this particular juncture, an analysis of the past could be more misleading than revealing when it comes to understanding the uniqueness of our day and the dangers of tomorrow.

Many historians will get their hackles up, and I cannot say I blame them. It is a wild idea. However, it is born of an analysis, not of straight lines or cyclical theory, but of mathematical exponentiality.

THE EXPONENTIAL CURVE

One major reason our problems today are unprecedented is because the mathematics are different. Many of the linear lines that in the past described our lives well have now disappeared. Replacing them are lines that slope upward exponentially.

Because there is little in our day-to-day lives that changes exponentially, we tend to think with a linear mind-set. The sun rises and the sun sets.

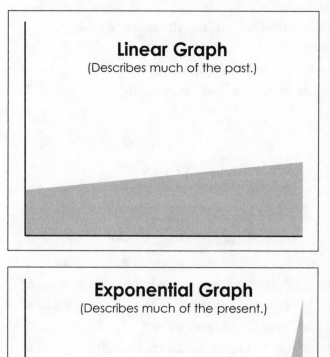

Linear Graph
(Describes much of the past.)

Exponential Graph
(Describes much of the present.)

Twenty-four hours is still only twenty-four hours. Week after week, everything seems about the same.

Meanwhile, largely unnoticed by us, history has shifted to fast forward. If linear still best describes our personal lives, exponential now best describes much of historical change. The significance of this is incalculable, yet the typical American, not knowing how to think in exponential terms, consistently underestimates it.

To illustrate how rapidly exponential numbers accumulate, consider the following exercise. If you fold a piece of paper in half forty times, how thick would it be? Thick enough to reach from here to the moon.

Such a result is more than unexpected—it is incomprehensible. This is why it is so hard to appreciate the radical dimensions of contemporary change. Yet incomprehensible or not, changes that follow an exponentially increasing curve are what we must now contend with, whether in total global information, complexity of systems, rapidity of change, gross national product, number of bankruptcies, cost of existing homes, cost of health care, cost of college education, number of prisoners, volume of e-mail, total number of Internet pages, volume of junk mail, volume of advertising, population of the world, life expectancy, explosive power of weaponry, etc. (See the Appendix). The circumstances of our age are quantitatively different from anything previously encountered, and the dramatic nature of this difference is consistently underestimated.

LIMITS

Because life has now shifted to exponential terms, the issue of limits has suddenly become an important one. We coast along for decades on the slow-growth portion of the exponential curve without encountering significant limit problems. Then, suddenly, we hit our head on the ceiling.

Previously, there was abundant margin in the world system, and we did not have to worry about limits. We could grow, expand, and waste as much as we wanted without worry. This is no longer the case. We have met or exceeded limits in scores of areas but don't know how to pull back. How do you slow a careening world when the throttle is stuck wide open?

All things have limits—people, governments, buildings, bridges, brains, and organizations. Even more subjective things such as friendships, creativity, or adaptability have limits. If we are well within boundaries, we can be expansive and growth-oriented. When approaching a limit, however, the rules change. Since we are impinging on many of these limits, much of our life experience is now traveling through uncharted territory. And because margin is closely related to the issue of limits, most of it has disappeared.

THE DISAPPEARANCE OF MARGIN

Whatever happened to margin? It was steamrolled by history. As noted, progress is a saboteur of margin. While margin can usually be counted upon to stay in one place, progress is always on the move—otherwise it would not be progress. After a time, progress turned over the speed controls to exponentiality, and we shifted into overdrive. Limits were hit with frightening suddenness.

Margin, the space that once existed between ourselves and our limits, was an early casualty. When you reach the limits of your resources or abilities, you have no margin left. So as history and progress picked up speed, we hit limit after limit. Slowly, margin began to disappear. Then when exponentiality took over the controls, margin vaporized.

Now that we have exceeded so many of our limits—personal, emotional, relational, physical, financial—we have no margin at all. Yet because we don't even know what margin is, we don't realize it is gone. We know that something is not right, but we can't solve the puzzle beyond that. Our pain is palpable, but our assailant remains unnamed.

Much of this pain is in our relational life: to self, to others, to God. We miss margin in many areas. But we require it in our relationships.

When we have no margin and our limits have been exceeded; when we are besieged by stress and overload; when our relational life is ailing; when it seems the flood of events is beyond our control; then problems take on a different dimension. One at a time they are perhaps manageable. But they just won't stand in line. Instead, they mound up suddenly and then bury us without warning.

4

THE PAIN OF STRESS

MANY OF THE annoyances of modernity do not yield to quick analysis. We wouldn't exactly label them evils—more like frustrations or nuisances. They are more like heartburn than homicide. You can't pick out a villain, yet you have a headache anyway. Sometimes you suspect there must be a computer virus hiding deep inside the center of the earth, clogging its gears. Maybe that's why so many things continue to backfire after all these years. Why can't the person using the sophisticated computer seem to clear up my magazine subscription? Why doesn't the IRS know the answers to its own questions? Whatever happened to friendly clerks? Why is it we don't feel confident that when the world awakens tomorrow, we will all be one day closer to victory?

YET ANOTHER POLLUTANT

High levels of stress follow as naturally after progress as does exhaust after traffic. It is a byproduct of our age, yet another societal pollutant. Pick up any periodical at the public library and see if it doesn't contain an article mentioning the subject. Four out of five Americans report a need to reduce stress in their lives, often resorting to tranquilizers. Why, in such a prosperous age, is it necessary to sedate so many? The negative aspects of stress disable the workplace as well, resulting in the loss of 225 million work days annually in the United States, nearly one million people for every working day.

OUR RESPONSE TO CHANGE

Dr. Hans Selye, the late Canadian endocrinologist and "father" of stress research, defines stress as "the nonspecific response of the body to any demand made upon it."[1] This definition is contrary to the popular thinking that defines stress as an unpleasant circumstance, such as tax time or a screaming baby. Stress is not the *circumstance*, it is our *response* to the circumstance.

It makes little difference if the situation we react to is positive or negative—both trigger the adaptational mechanism. Although the ultimate consequences of *frustrating stress* can be very different from those of *rewarding stress*, nevertheless, the initial adaptive response mechanism is similar in both cases. Merely encountering the word stress should not connote a positive or a negative feeling. The word only describes an entirely normal physiological process without which we would die.

Our bodies are constantly adapting to the environment. This adaptation is a marvelous process, more intricate than we imagine. A sophisticated organic communication network functions continuously at a low level. It is on perpetual alert, monitoring for changes in the environment. At times of increased need the system surges, preparing us for any necessary response.

This stress system is important and, in fact, vital. When overactive, however, damage can result. While stress itself need not be destructive, the overstimulation of an uncontrolled stress response may be both painful and destructive.

EUSTRESS, DISTRESS, HYPERSTRESS

Many of us, often without realizing it, use stress to our advantage. This *eustress*, or positive stress, energizes us. It is what football players call "psyching up" before a game. Eustress is what makes us especially creative before a deadline. It is what sleeping mothers use when they hear an infant gagging in the next room and they have to be instantly awake. This is what employers consciously induce in a work environment to make employees productive—a kind of creative tension. Some people love this feeling, thrive on it, and almost become addicted to it.

When the stress response becomes negative or destructive, it is called *distress*. This is what most of us mean when we use the word stress. We are really referring to the negative aspects of stress, or distress.

An excessive volume of stress is called *hyperstress*. The volume is important because how we deal with stress depends on how much of it we are confronted with. If the amounts are manageable, we can learn to avoid distress and possibly turn it into eustress. If, however, the amounts are at hyperstress levels, then stress reduction is more important than stress management.

If the stress reaction is resolved successfully, no apparent damage is noticed. If, however, the result is failure or frustration, multiple pathologies may ensue: tissue aging occurs at the cellular level; the immune system may malfunction; cardiovascular catastrophes, such as stroke or heart attack, may occur.

Is It Worse Today?

Stress has been called a national epidemic. Is it a modern disease? Haven't people always had stresses? The answer to both questions is yes. Humankind has always had problems, and many of them were caused by stress. Yet our current stress plague differs dramatically from the experience of our ancestors. Conditions of modern living overstimulate our stress response more than in previous times, and many of the issues are too complex for successful resolution.

"But look at the statistics," you protest. "Infant mortality is down and life expectancy is up. We have one of the highest standards of living in the world. The elderly have Social Security and Medicare, while the poor have food stamps and Medicaid." Yes, and we all have stress. It is woven as tightly into the fabric of modern life as is television.

No one in the history of humankind has ever had to live with the number and intensity of stressors we have acting upon us today. They are unprecedented. The human spirit is called upon to withstand rapid changes and pressures never before encountered.

Physical Stress, Mental Stress

Our stress problem is further clarified by examining the difference between physical and mental pressures. Biochemical stress parameters are more affected by psychological stressors than by physical stressors. Physical hard work, for example, is not really a stressor at all, as long as one has some control over it. A person can work twelve hours a day, six days a week for an entire life at physical labor and suffer no ill effects—as long as that person has decision-control over the work schedule. Actually, such hard physical labor would usually have salutary health benefits. But if the strain is mental and a person is constantly being frustrated, the negative health effects can be catastrophic.

In one study, a patient was first given a cardiac treadmill exam. Despite vigorous physical exercise, the patient's cardiovascular status remained normal throughout. He then was asked to subtract seven from 777 serially for three-and-one-half minutes. His blood pressure went up forty points. Similar results have been achieved in other studies. Certain biochemical stress parameters are more affected by psychological stressors than by physical stressors. Chronic uncertainty, sustained levels of increased vigilance, or struggling with a mental task are more stressful than chopping wood.

"The widespread substitution of mental strain for physical strain is no advantage from our point of view," maintained E. F. Schumacher. "Proper physical work, even if strenuous, does not absorb a great deal of the power of attention, but mental work does; so that there is no attention left over for the spiritual things that really matter. It is obviously much easier for a hard-working peasant to keep his mind attuned to the divine than ror a strained office worker."[2]

SPICE OF LIFE, KISS OF DEATH

Individuals differ significantly regarding how much stress is desirable or what types of events are distressing. What strains some does not bother others. I, for example, do not mind waiting in lines but don't enjoy going to formal parties. Another person might react the opposite—despising lines but loving parties. A stressor that for one might be pleasure, for another might be pain. For one, the spice of life; for another, the kiss of death.

Some people desire a low level of stress to feel comfortable. Our modern pace was not particularly designed with them in mind. Others seek a high, almost frenzied level of stress and seem to thrive on it. Different stressors, different personalities, different results. Let's look at some of these categories.

Type A—The type A personality is commonly characterized as "driven." Type As have a drive to control others, an aggressiveness and competitiveness characterized by a need to win. They think multiple thoughts and do multiple actions at the same time. Margin is not a priority to preserve but a gap to be filled.

These hardworking, time-pressured individuals are more prone to cardiovascular disease. Their carburetors are set on high, and they surge into overdrive at the slightest provocation. Most people find a vacation relaxing, but type As often do not. Relaxing is one of the most stressful things on their agenda, which is why they seldom do it. Progress and type As feed on each other. They are very productive people and usually the leaders of companies or institutions. But they live on a high level of stress and have significant health problems because of it.

The Extrovert or Introvert—The introvert is a personality type vulnerable to the stresses of the crowd. Introverts like to be alone. They appreciate quiet, solitude, and time to think and feel in their own internal world.

They generally do not like having a large number of social interactions or going to parties.

The majority of Americans, however, are extroverts, and extroverts are energized by such social exchange. Extroverts usually don't understand introverts and try to push them into situations where they simply don't wish to be.

The Depressed or Anxious—Another group of people in a special stress category are those who have generalized depression or anxiety. *Depression* is the feeling that life is painful and hopeless. *Anxiety* is the looming belief that circumstances *will imminently become* painful and hopeless. Whether depressed, anxious, or both, these people feel pressure from stressors that are inflated or perhaps not even there at all.

Some, for example, are always stressed when they ride in a car. They have never been in an accident but are fearful that today will be the day. Every car they pass along the route, therefore, becomes a stressor. These anxious and/or depressed people will be burdened much of their lives simply because they perceive stressors as more of a threat than they really are. One important lesson emerges from such an illustration: Often our perception of the stressor damages us more than the stressor itself.

The Elderly—Evidence indicates that mental stressors induce more tension in the elderly than in the young. Performing serial seven subtraction is only mildly stressful for those in their twenties. Many elderly, however, are hyper responsive to such stimuli and become agitated in performing the task.

Children—Pediatricians, child psychologists, and developmental experts all believe that our current age is more stressful for children. Social change is too rapid, competition is too stiff, and expectations have risen too high. *Time* magazine ran an article titled "Burning Out at Nine?"[3] followed a few years later by *Newsweek*'s contribution titled "The Overscheduled Baby."[4] Added to the host of already oppressive burdens are children's insecurities about family stability. Children have a great stake in whether their parents stay together or not, but little control over the matter.

CONTEMPORARY STRESSORS

Avoiding all stress is as impossible as it is undesirable. It is *impossible* because modern living challenges us continuously with adaptational demands. It is *undesirable* because a stress-free life—no change, no challenge, no novelty—is literally fatal. Even a low-stress life, that often sounds so attractive, is consistently described as "boring." But neither do we want *hyperstress*.

Where does this leave us? Human performance does best, and even thrives, if we can keep the amount of change and stress in our lives within an acceptable range of tolerances. Unfortunately, for many of us, we exceed this range routinely and chronic hyperstress has become the new normal.

Our stress diet selects from a diverse menu. The following are some of the most prominent items.

Change—Do not underestimate it. We pay a price for each change we must adapt to. The Life Change Index is one scale that quantifies change and assigns a corresponding health risk: The greater the change, the higher the risk.

Mobility—Mobility is a subset of change. People move, for the most part, because of perceived advantages. Each move, however, entails an adaptation to the new environment (which is stressful) plus a severing of old ties (also stressful).

Expectations—Modernity has increased our expectations but has not always permitted a commensurate ability to meet them. Frustration results.

Time pressure—The clock dominates our schedule as never before. We have more activities to arrive at and more deadlines to meet. Most of us are all too familiar with the feeling of panic as an appointed hour nears with work yet undone. We are ruled not by the week or day but by the minute.

Work—For many, distress and work are the same word. There is, for example, the Boston obstetrician who left his practice and opened a laundromat. Or the commercial airline pilot who, after waiting to take off, taxied back to the terminal, walked off the plane, and quit. We change jobs more frequently, and we rotate more shifts. We have many more deadlines yet less control.

Control—Stress can be successfully managed if we have control over what is happening. If the situation is beyond our influence, however, frustration leads to mental or physical damage.

Fear—Some researchers believe fear to be the root cause of all stress reaction. We have many reasons for our insecurities: pressured deadlines, fragile job futures, economic vulnerability, loss of control, conditional relationships, overloaded lives.

Relationships—The intact, supportive relationships we all require for healthy living have dissipated under the tutelage of progress. The family has been systematically dismantled, and at the same time, long-term friendships are increasingly rare.

Competition—Modern life has become essentially a comparative—and even hypercompetitive—experience. The winners excel while the multitude of losers try to deal with the stress of not measuring up.

Frustration, anger—Perhaps the greatest emotional stressors are frustration and anger. These block our ability to use stress in a positive manner and virtually assure destructive results at some level.

It is important to understand the effect of combined stressors, for the whole is greater than the sum of the parts. We might be able to adapt successfully to one or two assaults on our internal response mechanism, but when six or eight major stressors compound the challenge, our chances of success are diminished.

BROKENNESS AND BURNOUT

The effects of stress disorders are noticed in three spheres: psychological, physical, and behavioral. Burnout is a pervasive disturbance in all three areas.

Psychological Symptoms—Most people are aware of the link between stress and our psychological well-being. The psyche, it seems, is the most common point of entry for the stress virus, with symptoms including:

depression, withdrawal, apathy, mental fatigue, anxiety, feeling that things are slipping out of control, negative thinking, difficulty making decisions, exaggerated worrying, anger and hostility, impatience, forgetfulness, and confusion.

Physical Symptoms—Our response to stressors takes place not only at the thought level but also at the organ and even the cellular level. Such physical symptoms include: rapid pulse, palpitations, increased blood pressure, hyperacidity, ulcers, irritable bowel, tightening of the muscles, headaches, weight changes, compromised immune system, unexplained fatigue, rashes, itching, insomnia, and shortness of breath.

Behavioral Symptoms—What our mind and body experience, our behaviors often express. If, for example, we are psychologically depressed and physically exhausted, we will begin to act in a manner consistent with these symptoms. These behaviors include: irritation with friends and colleagues, bossiness, outbursts of temper, withdrawal and detachment, sudden tears, changes in eating or sleeping patterns or in the sexual drive, accident proneness, reckless driving, inappropriate laughter, compulsive shopping, increased use of tranquilizers, alcohol, or cigarettes.

Burnout—If you bend a small tree and then release it, the sapling will return to its former shape. This is analogous to stress—we bend and then recover. However, if you bend the sapling until it snaps, it stays broken. This is analogous to burnout. Something inside breaks. Common burnout phrases include: "I dread going to work," "I can't stand this any more," "I'd rather be alone," "I don't care," "I hate it!" "I want out of here!" Of course, there can be and usually is, healing following burnout. A return to passion, enthusiasm, and full productivity often occurs. But the healing takes a long time and is mostly by scar formation, while the co-morbidity is very high.

A DOSE OF MARGIN

Some in our midst quickly grow impatient with all this stress talk and would instead challenge the weak to quit all the whining and get with the program. They love stress and seem to thrive on marginless living. The driven live on the edge and wouldn't have it any other way. They eat, breathe, and sleep adrenaline. Productivity is the goal, not living. Margin is a hole to be plugged as quickly as possible.

Yet even these racehorses have their limits, as they will eventually learn. And when they do, I hope they will not underestimate the stress-reducing value of taking a dose of margin against the pain.

THE PAIN OF OVERLOAD

"IT HURTS," SAID David Tate. As a mere 180-pound member of the Chicago Bears' defensive secondary, one would think he was discussing taking a hit on the playing field. Instead, the pain comes from being "splashed" in the 1990 Bears' "Locker Room Wars."

The Bears' huge defensive linemen and the smaller defensive backs had a good-natured but weighty battle of intimidation going on. Following an exchange of verbal assaults, the big guys start moving, trying to circle and isolate one of the "Brat Pack." On most occasions, the smaller, faster defensive backs are able to strike and quickly escape. But if captured, they pay a huge price. Tate was dropped to the ground and the 320-pound William "Refrigerator" Perry collapsed on top of him. Then 270-pound Richard Dent, 275-pound Dan Hampton, and 270-pound Steve McMichael jumped on top—1,135 pounds of pain.

"I don't think they know how heavy they are," said Tate. "Once you've gotten splashed, you avoid it at all costs—even if it means backing down."

"Splashing" is perhaps the consummate picture of overload. Overloading is a painful occurrence. Yet, in one form or another, it happens daily to nearly every one of us.

A Matter of Thresholds

The spontaneous tendency of our culture is to inexorably add detail to our lives: one more option, one more commitment, one more expectation, one more purchase, one more debt, one more change, one more job, one more decision. We must now deal with more "things per person" than at any other time in history. Yet one can comfortably handle only so many details in his or her life. Exceeding this threshold will result in disorganization or frustration. It is important to note here that the problem is not in the "details." The problem is in the "exceeding." This is called overloading.

Overloading occurs whenever the requirements upon us exceed that which we are able to bear. For example, camels are able to carry great loads. If, however, a straw is placed on a camel maximally loaded down, its back will be broken. The back is not broken by the straw; it was broken by overload.

The Law of Limits

As we have already discussed, all systems have limits. Human beings are systems, and as such have physical, performance, emotional, and mental limits. To understand the concept of overloading, it is helpful to understand the law of limits, for overloading is a phenomenon of limits. "Researchers," according to sociologist Alvin Toffler, "strongly agree on two basic principles: first, that man has limited capacity; and second, that overloading the system leads to serious breakdown of performance."[1]

Physical Limits are the easiest to recognize. A room can hold only so much furniture. We might put ten pieces of furniture in the room and possibly even thirty. But we would not try to put one thousand tables and chairs in a room too small to hold them. This would overload the room in a visibly foolish way.

To cite another example, engineers study stress loads when designing bridges, and we often see the sign "Load Limit Ahead" as we approach such a bridge. A forty-ton truck would not attempt to cross a bridge limited to twenty-ton vehicles. Because such physical limits are visible and measurable, humans do not commonly overload in these areas. Few attempt to swim the Pacific Ocean or to climb the stairs of the Sears Tower.

Performance Limits are related to physical limits but also introduce the factor of will. The endpoint is not as objectively defined, and we often are not quite as willing to accept the fact that there are limits. This is where stress fractures come from—people want to push themselves beyond the limit of breakdown.

Sleep might serve as another example. We all need sleep. But how much? Those who regard the need for sleep as a sign of weakness might try to push the limit and see how few hours they can get along on. Four hours a night? Three? You can sleep three hours a night, but you are impinging on a limit and there will be consequences.

The human function curve (figure 5.1) illustrates the principle well. Our performance increases with increasing demand and increasing effort— but only up to a point. Once we reach our limit, fatigue sets in, followed quickly by exhaustion and collapse.

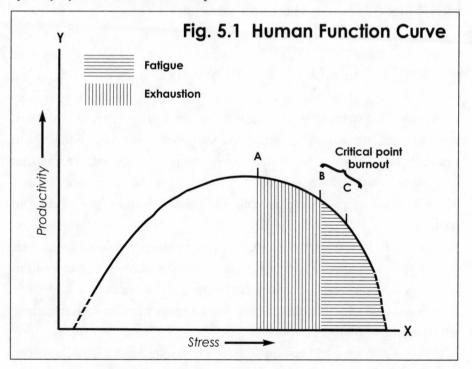

Fig. 5.1 Human Function Curve

Emotional Limits are even more vague. How much straining can the psyche withstand before being overloaded? Physically, most of us could carry a one-hundred-pound person on our back. But we could not carry ten. We would not even try. What is clear to us in the context of physical limits is less clear regarding emotional limits. To extend the analogy of carrying people into the emotional context, you might be able to emotionally "carry" one person. But what about five? Ten? One hundred? Where should we draw the line?

The limits of emotional overloading are hard to define, and helping people is one of the easiest places where emotional overload is manifested. "In a culture where whirl is king, we must understand our emotional limits," asserts Richard Foster. "Ulcers, migraines, nervous tension, and a dozen other symptoms mark our psychic overload. We are concerned not to live beyond our means financially; why do it emotionally?"[2]

Mental Limits are as difficult to define as emotional limits, but the existence of such limits is indisputable. Information overload soon results in mental short-circuiting. The memory banks are full, and the mind shuts down for a rest. Air-traffic controllers are a prime example of too much mental stress too fast, and burnout on this job is routine.

"I CAN DO ALL THINGS . . ."

In running and swimming, we continue to break old records nearly every year. Runners keep running faster, and swimmers keep swimming faster. But there must be an end to this, true? We cannot run the mile in one second. Neither will it ever be possible for anyone to run it in one minute. There is a built-in physiological limit beyond which records will rarely be broken.

So it is in life. We are not infinite. The day does not have more than twenty-four hours. We do not have an inexhaustible source of human energy. We cannot keep running on empty. Limits are real, and despite what some stoics might think, limits are not even an enemy. Overloading is the enemy.

Some will respond: "I can do all things through Christ who strengthens me."[3] Does this mean that you can fly? Can you go six months without eating? Neither can you live a healthy life chronically overloaded. God did not intend this verse to represent a negation of life-balance. Even Jesus Himself did not heal every case of leprosy in Israel. Think about it.

It is God the Creator who made limits, and it is the same God who placed them within us for our protection. We exceed them at our peril.

LIMITS AND THE SATURATION POINT

Often we do not feel overload sneaking up on us. We instead feel energized by the rapidity of events and the challenge of our full days. Then one day we find it difficult to get out of bed. Life has become a weight. Perhaps it is in our parenting that we feel exhausted. Perhaps it is that second job we took to pay for the new car. Or perhaps we can't bear to hear of yet one more people problem.

What happened to change our enthusiasm to pain? Not all threshold limits are appreciated as we near them, and it is only in exceeding them that we suddenly feel the breakdown.

When our lives are saturated, we should tread carefully. Have you been there? It is similar to the straw that broke the camel's back. The camel was doing fine until . . . Most times we seem to be bearing up fine under the heavy load, but then something snaps.

When you feel such a snap, understand it for what it is. Don't blame your work, your friends, or your children. Blame overload.

EVERYWHERE AND INESCAPABLE

While working at a hospital in central India I observed that poverty was omnipresent and inescapable. The poor were at the train station, alongside the road, and on every city street. Even the wealthiest people could not isolate themselves from the presence of poverty.

Overload in the United States is similar to poverty in India. It is everywhere and it is inescapable. Everyone I know suffers from overload in at least some form. For one person it might be traffic overload, for another change overload, and for a third it might be expectation overload. For most of us, it is a combination of multiple overloads, configured according to the context of our individual lives. Wherever we go, the syndrome has gone before us. It is not chosen. It is simply a part of living, compliments of progress.

THE VARIED WAYS WE HURT

Despite its universality, the syndrome manifests itself differently in each person. Also, each person has a different tolerance. The threshold point where breakdown begins to occur varies from person to person. But I have not yet met a person who could tolerate ever-escalating overload without eventually feeling its painful weight.

If the overloaded seek professional help, what kinds of manifestations might the counselors discover? Some victims of overload experience *anxiety.* The load is simply too much to manage, and tranquilizers are a hoped-for solution. If the load is not lightened soon, however, breakdown can occur. "When our bodies and feelings can't cope any longer with the demands made upon them, when the overload becomes too great, their only course of action is to shut everything down," explains Robert Banks. "For many people, physical or nervous breakdown is the only way out of the impasse."[4]

Others manifest *hostility,* blaming their overload on those around them. The nightly news details the results: shootings on the freeway due to traffic overload; rudeness in big cities blamed on people overload; brawls in the NBA because of competition overload.

Some personality types lapse into *depression* when overloaded. They might feel hostile, but the hostility is directed inward. Having failed their own expectations and the expectations of others, they withdraw into a fog of gloom.

Many develop *resentment,* often toward their jobs. They might love their work, but overload turns work into an enemy. A physician friend was recently lamenting his continual twelve-hour days. "No, your ulcer isn't bleeding," he moaned silently while listening to the patient describe his stomach pain. "It can't be. It just can't be!"

Easily Misdiagnosed

Because the overload syndrome expresses itself differently in different people, we must be careful with our judgments. Misdiagnosis is common. In fact, I would say that misdiagnosis is the rule. The overload syndrome is often inaccurately labeled weakness, apathy, or lack of commitment.

For example, I recently read an article critical of the phrase, "I'm too busy." The author, a nationally known spiritual leader, was quite upset at hearing this excuse so frequently. Saying you're too busy is the perfect cover, he wrote, because the pretense of busyness is difficult to counter. After all, how can someone tell you, "No, you aren't too busy. You're just using that as an excuse"? The excuse of busyness, he concluded, is actually the problem of not caring enough.

There is obvious frustration here, but in many cases his accusation will have missed the diagnosis. The problem is indeed busyness, not apathy. The problem is overload. It is real, and it is here to stay. Let's blame it, not each other.

Each of us needs to seek his or her own level of involvement and not let the standard be mandated by the often exorbitant expectations of others. Some around us who are much more involved than we are may not understand why we choose to hold back. Others might be much less involved than we are—we assume they don't care. We must understand that everyone has a different tolerance for overload and a different threshold level when breakdown begins to occur. It is important for us to set people free to seek their own level.

When given this freedom, some unfortunately will indeed use the overload principle as an excuse for laziness. Exploitation will occur by those who claim to be overloaded but instead are simply undisciplined. In this case I may wish to employ a large measure of grace as I talk to them about their level of involvement. But as soon as I condemn them or try to control them, I violate who they are before God. Making them accountable to Him does not mean that they must then do as I wish them to do. My own spiritual walk in the midst of my own overload is enough of a burden to keep me fully occupied.

In my experience, the greater problem in our society is not the lack of accountability but the desire to control other people's lives. It is better to not judge the sluggard than it is to mistakenly judge the already over-loaded. When people are overloaded, the last thing they need is the additional burden of our reproof. So if we err, at least let us err on the side of grace.

UNPRECEDENTED

Hasn't overload always been with us? No.

An important thesis of this book is that we live in an unprecedented age. Our modern day is not only qualitatively different from any other but also quantitatively different. Future history books will need to use a different vocabulary to describe contemporary phenomena, and prominent among these words will be "exponential," "limits," "thresholds," and "overload."

Overload is a matter of mathematics, and today's math computes differently. Life, change, history—all are unfolding exponentially. Threshold limits are being reached with frightening suddenness. Overload is happening overnight.

Many people, however, are trapped in a linear paradigm, a mind-set that can only see straight ahead. While they understand our qualitative changes, they have failed to comprehend the quantitative nature of "future shock." As long as this is the case, the reasons for our contemporary problems will remain invisible to them.

SPECIFICS OF THE SYNDROME

The following are abbreviated discussions of the overload syndrome in its varied manifestations.

Activity overload—Booked up weeks in advance, we are a busy people. In an attempt to squeeze more things in, we try to do two or three at the same time. Activity overload takes away the pleasure of anticipation and the delight of reminiscence.

Change overload—For millennia upon millennia, change was slow, controlled, assessable; now it convulses at warp speed. "Nothing defines our age more than the furious and relentless increase in the rate of change," summarizes historian Arthur M. Schlesinger, Jr.[5]

Choice overload—In 1980, there were 12,000 items in the average supermarket; today there are 30,000—including the 186 different choices of breakfast cereal in our local grocery store. Purchase a satellite dish and choose from 1,100 movies every month. "As the number of choices grows further," writes sociology professor Barry Schwartz in *The Paradox of Choice,* "the negatives escalate until we become overloaded. At this point, choice no longer liberates but debilitates. It might even be said to tyrannize."[6]

Commitment overload—Most of us have more commitments than time. "Some people can't say no," observes Dr. J. Grant Howard. "They take on too many relationships and too many responsibilities. They enroll in too many courses, hold down too many jobs, volunteer for too many tasks, make too many appointments, serve on too many committees, have too many friends. They are trying to be all things to all men all at once all by themselves."[7]

Debt overload—Currently every sector of society is awash in red ink. Concerning our national debt, complained one senator, "We're institutionally incapable of saying No." In our foreign trade deficit, we are the world's largest debtor nation. Corporate and personal consumer debt levels function more like anchors than catalysts.

Decision overload—Every year we have more decisions to make and less time to make them. The small decisions don't cost us much: Which soda? Which pizza toppings? Mint toothpaste or tartar control gel? But along with these trivial decisions come a myriad of other choices that are not at all easy: whether or not to have children and how many; whether to move or change jobs; whether both spouses should work outside the home; whether to put Grandma into the nursing home. Trivial or tough, having too many decisions to make in too short a time is vintage overload.

Expectation overload—A clear result of our affluent communications age is the steady rising of expectations. "Your world should know no boundaries," advertises one investment firm. "If you can dream it, you can do it. Now there's no limit to your ability," claims an insurance company.

Fatigue overload—We are a tired society. Even our leisure is exhausting—54 percent of us admit we are more exhausted at the end of a vacation than at the beginning. With generator indicators continuously pointing to "discharge," it is little wonder our batteries are drained. Our weary, withered state is not God's plan. Fatigue overload attacks our emotions, leaving us self-protective; it attacks our bodies, leaving us weak; and it attacks our relationships, leaving us isolated. That we are fatigued is not the fault of activities or friends—it is the fault of overload.

Hurry overload—Haste is a modern ailment. Our lives are nonstop, lived at a breathless pace. We walk fast, talk fast, eat fast, and then excuse ourselves by saying, "I must run." Thirty-six percent of us say we are rushed all the time. But, as the Finnish proverb teaches, God did not create hurry.

Information overload—A single edition of the *New York Times* contains more information than a seventeenth-century Britisher would encounter in a lifetime. If I read two health articles every day, next year I would be eight centuries behind in my reading. We are buried by data on a daily basis.

Media overload—Ninety-nine percent of American homes have television, with the average set turned on fifty-five hours a week. Televised news is 24/7. We buy more books per capita than ever before and can choose from 63,000 new titles every year. How does one read a three-and-one-half-inch thick Sunday paper?

Noise overload—Noise has become one of the most universal forms of pollution in the industrial world. Every day 50 percent of the U.S. population is exposed to noise that interferes with speech or sleep. True quiet is extremely rare.

People overload—"I would rather sit on a pumpkin and have it all to myself, than be crowded on a velvet cushion," wrote Henry David Thoreau. Personally, as a fellow introvert, I agree with him. But such is not the world we live in. God has given us people to love and serve. Billions of them. Each of us is exposed to a greater number of people than ever before. Socialization and community are wonderful. Unfortunately, crowding often leads to depersonalization and rudeness.

Possession overload—We have more "things per person" than any other nation in history. Closets are full, storage space is used up, and cars can't fit into garages. Having first imprisoned us with debt, possessions then take over our houses and occupy our time. This begins to sound like an invasion. Everything I own owns me. Why would I want more?

Technology overload—It has been estimated that the average person must learn to operate twenty thousand pieces of equipment. Some elicit our gratitude, others our exasperation. I, for example, have a physics degree but don't know how to set my watch.

Traffic overload—Roadways are called "clogways," our national flower has become the cloverleaf, and rush hour is neither rush nor an hour. We now have more cars per family than drivers per family. The word travel comes originally from *travail*, and we are rediscovering its true meaning.

Work overload—Work is God-ordained. Work overload, however, was not part of the original plan. Yet every morning millions of Americans head drudgingly to an exhausting work schedule that leaves them stressed and worn out. The earlier predictions of shorter work-weeks and higher incomes have backfired. Instead we often find total family work schedules exceeding eighty hours a week—yet another family "over-working and under-relating."

WHY DO WE DO IT?

If overloading causes such widespread social and personal dysfunction, why do we do it?

One reason is lack of understanding. Because it is a relatively new phenomenon, we don't see overload even when it has us by the throat.

Second, some accept overload uncritically because of conscientiousness. "It is our duty to do all that we can," they reason. But how does one define "all that we can"? A line must be drawn this side of overload if we are to stay healthy. Drawing such a line causes the overly conscientious to feel guilt. I appreciate those who have this sense of duty. Nevertheless, chronic overloading is not God's will. It is okay to draw a line.

Yet a third dynamic that inflicts overload on many unwilling victims is "follow the leader." Our economy and our society are run by the driven. They climb to positions of power by force and then demand the same overcommitment from those under them. That our leaders should require of us an honest day's work is not disputed. But when they require overloading that destroys the worker, then they have exceeded the moral mandate for leadership.

In all that precedes, I am not suggesting that we should strive to have a pain-free, stress-free life. The Christian walk will always be full of problems and work. Many times we must be prepared to suffer willingly. What I am suggesting, however, is that given the ubiquity of overload, we need to choose carefully where our involvement should come. We must not allow ourselves to be hammered by distress in the many areas of life that have absolutely no transcendent importance. It is not the will of the Father for us to be so battered by the torment of our age. There must be a different way—a way that reserves our strength for higher battles. And indeed there is.

SETTING LIMITS

To date, people do not operate on the principle of overloading. Instead, they operate on the basis of "one more thing won't hurt." Yet this is only true if it is true. Once we are maximally loaded down, adding one more thing will hurt. The pain of overload is real pain.

Chronic overloading also has a negative effect on our spiritual lives.

We have less time for prayer and meditation, less energy for service, and less interest in relationship.

If we don't move to establish effective priorities, overloading will continue to fill up our schedules and keep us captive. We must learn the art of setting limits. We must learn to accept the finality and nonnegotiability of the twenty-four-hour day. We must learn not to overdraw on our account of emotional energy. And we must learn to respect such limits in others.

Margin can teach us these things. Margin can restore to us that which has been taken away. It is an idea whose time has come.

PART TWO

THE PRESCRIPTION

MARGIN

MARGIN

DESPITE ITS TIMELINESS, few people are aware of the concept of margin. Not that the concept is inconsequential. Indeed, it is compellingly important. Nor is the concept difficult to understand. Rather, the reason margin has not become a household word is simply because it has not yet been properly introduced.

It is now time. For if today margin is useful, tomorrow it will be urgent. If today it is valuable, tomorrow it will be essential.

Although some people seem capable of thriving without margin, most of us find it a prerequisite for well-being. Margin grants freedom and permits rest. It nourishes both relationship and service. Spiritually, it allows availability for the purposes of God. From a medical point of view, it is health-enhancing. It is a welcome addition to our health formulary: Add a dose of margin and see if life doesn't come alive once again.

THE OPPOSITE OF OVERLOAD

Margin is the space between our load and our limits. It is the amount allowed beyond that which is needed. It is something held in reserve for contingencies or unanticipated situations. Margin is the gap between rest and exhaustion, the space between breathing freely and suffocating.

Margin is the opposite of overload. If we are overloaded we have no margin. Most people are not quite sure when they pass from margin to overload. Threshold points are not easily measurable and are also different for different people in different circumstances. We don't want to be under-achievers (heaven forbid!), so we fill our schedules uncritically. Options are as attractive as they are numerous, and we overbook.

If we were equipped with a flashing light to indicate "100 percent full," we could better gauge our capacities. But we don't have such an indicator light, and we don't know when we have overextended until we feel the pain. As a result, many people commit to a 120 percent life and wonder why the burden feels so heavy. It is rare to see a life prescheduled to only 80 percent, leaving a margin for responding to the unexpected that God sends our way.

Power Minus Load

The formula for margin is straightforward: Power – Load = Margin.

Power is made up of factors such as energy, skills, time, training, emotional and physical strength, faith, finances, and social supports.

Load is made up of such factors as work, problems, obligations and commitments, expectations (internal and external), debt, deadlines, and interpersonal conflicts.

When our load is greater than our power, we enter into negative margin status, that is, we are overloaded. Endured long-term, this is not a healthy state. Severe negative margin for an extended period of time is another name for burnout.

When our power is greater than the load, however, we have margin. Even a cursory examination of this formula reveals that to increase margin one needs to simply increase power or decrease load—or both.

Given that the formula is simple and the consequences of living without margin are painful, why is the concept not universally understood? The answer reveals a principle: not all societal pathogens are equally visible. The causes of some pains are more readily apparent than others.

THE SEMIVISIBLE

If starving or thirsty, we needn't be told that food or water is what we lack. If sleep-deprived, we needn't be told that sleep is what we yearn for. If exhausted from a thirty-mile walk, we needn't be told that rest is what our body craves. If bankrupt, we needn't be told that money is what we require.

Why, then, when we so desperately need margin in our lives, is it necessary to explain our need for it? Why don't we understand it by instinct?

In answering this question, it is helpful to note that some burdens and pains in life are visible while others are not. "Visible" means that they can be perceived with one of the five senses or they can be quantified or measured. For example, if you smash your finger with a hammer, you don't have to guess about what hurts or why. Physical pains are obvious and visible. In much the same way, financial pains are usually visible.

Other pains, however, cannot be perceived by the senses in quite the same way; neither can they be measured or quantified. They are invisible or, perhaps more accurately, semivisible. Emotional, psychological, social, relational, and spiritual pains often fit this description. The pain is real, to be sure. But the details of cause and effect are hard to sort out.

In this same way, margin is semivisible. Living without it does not cause a sensory pain, but instead a deep-seated subjective ache. Because the ache and heaviness are only semivisible, the pain of marginless living is hard for us to talk about. We feel guilty and weak if we complain. We feel vulnerable to the slings and arrows of the contemptuously stoical. It is hard to justify our inner pains when we don't have a vocabulary to use.

Living without margin has, to date, been unseen and unexplained — but not unfelt. Yet it is not buried so deeply that we must send the philosophers out to find it. Instead, it is common and universal enough that even a simple family doctor can explain the concept. And once explained, the fog lifts.

Very seldom do people attempt to refute the diagnosis. Instead, most say, "So that's the problem!" It's as if a switch is tripped in their understanding. Instantly, they have hope that their burden is finally being understood.

A MATTER OF THRESHOLDS

To further illustrate how this historical process of discovery happens, let's look briefly at the beginnings of stress research. Stress is similar to margin; both are threshold phenomena (a certain overloading limit must be reached before the consequences are felt) and both are semivisible (the causes are not readily apparent). Understanding how the awareness of stress was brought to light will help us to understand how this same process is now happening to margin.

Our great-grandparents did not go around complaining about how "stressed" they were. As a matter of fact, no one talked much about stress until at least the 1950s for it wasn't until then that the concept was published by Dr. Selye. Now, however, every American knows about stress. People throw around the term as if it has always been a given. Most of us still do not know how to quantify stress—it's semivisible. But no one tries to refute it any more.

Stress is a threshold phenomenon. Until a certain level of change and adaptational demand was reached, no one was aware of it. Once that threshold was exceeded, however, stress was explained, understood, applied, and then canonized.

Margin is also a threshold phenomenon. Just as *stress* and *change* are related, so *margin* and *load* are related. But margin did not appear on our pain agenda until a certain threshold was reached, namely until the "more and more of everything faster and faster" of progress collided with human limits. At precisely that point, load became overload. And, at the same moment, our margin disappeared.

It is not that we need margin today but never had need of it before. We have always needed it. It is as basic a necessity as rest. It's just that the threshold had never been reached before, allowing us to discover our need.

Margin is simply an idea whose time has come—nothing more and nothing less. It is simple, fundamental, and easily accessible. And it is a friend whose company we would be wise to cultivate.

MARGIN: YESTERYEAR'S CHARM?

Margin was an unrecognized possession of the peoples of the past. Throughout most of the history of the world, margin existed in the lives of individuals as well as societies. There were no televisions to watch or phones to answer. There were no cars, and travel was seldom undertaken. Daily newspapers were unknown. The media could not broadcast the cluster of events taking place in town. Churches and communities did not offer twenty simultaneous programs. With no electricity to extend daylight, few suffered sleep deprivation. Time urgency, daily planners, and to-do lists had not yet been adopted by the masses.

Instead, by default rather than choice, people lived slower, more deliberate lives. They had time to help a neighbor. Their church and social activities more often drew them together than pulled them apart. The past might have been poor and deprived in many respects, but its people had margin.

Perhaps this is a key to understanding why the past often holds such charm. Surely we overrate its positives and, at the same time, overlook the hardships. Yet, one suspects there must be at least *some* substance to our widespread nostalgia. Those who dismiss the feelings of fondness we have for the past with a haughty sweep of the hand are not being careful enough.

It is intriguing to postulate that margin might be the unsuspected link. Without even knowing exactly what it is that we miss, we miss margin. As progress arrives, margin dissipates. Progress devours margin, and we yearn to have it back.

THE THIRD WORLD'S REMAINING TREASURE

To test this hypothesis, we might compare life as it was lived in our past and the lifestyle we observe in developing countries today. Conditions in Third-World countries are sad in many respects and often heart-rending. But after working in many of these countries, I am struck by the recurring impression that the people have margin. They sit and visit, they watch children play, they walk without hurry, and they sleep full nights.

Talk to those who have spent time in such developing countries and see what they report. True, life there is often frustrating—and sometimes completely exasperating. Many of the modern conveniences are distressingly absent. But the slower pace is consistently commented upon, and almost always with affection.

Good friends of ours returned to the States after doing medical work in Mali, West Africa. They don't miss the sand and heat, the scorpions and insects, the hepatitis and malaria. But they do miss Mali. Why? They miss their friends and the work there . . . and they miss their margin. Every evening, for example, the family retired to the courtyard of their home where Mom pitched, Dad fielded, and the boys ran the bases. When this family returned to the States, their margin vanished about ten milliseconds after the plane touched down.

From across the continent comes a similar story: "I think back to the nine years our family enjoyed on the lower slopes of the Kilimanjaro in East Africa. There, while our work was sometimes tense, the pace surely resembled more a walk than a run. There were plenty of green trees to sit under and a conscience that allowed us to sit down under them," comments former missionary Mildred Tengbom. "We weren't constantly being told that our value depended on how 'active' or 'involved' we were."[1]

More evidence of African margin comes from a surgeon who spent one year there.

All things considered I would have to say that it was much healthier for me living overseas. There are stresses, of course, but of a much different type and magnitude. . . .

Although I do not consider myself a "workaholic," I do find it difficult to control the time I spend in my practice. Still, I thought I was reasonably happy until I found out how beneficial a 'sabbatical' in Africa can be. . . . I wasn't exactly loafing, since I did nearly five hundred operations in that year, but I still had large amounts of free time to read, rest and play. . . .

In the absence of television, telephones and shopping centers, the inner life gets some long-needed attention. . . . I often had time for a midday nap, to eat almost all meals with my family, and to enjoy having evenings and weekends relatively free as well. With a swimming hole nearby, complete with vine swing, and surrounded by a gorgeous tropical rain forest, we could always find fun things to do. . . . We played table games, assembled puzzles together, read nearly thirty books aloud, and did creative things such as handcrafts and art. . . . The leisure time also afforded the opportunity to meditate, listen to God more, and reflect on priorities and the direction my life should take.[2]

ISLAND LIVING

Several years ago, after the American intervention of 1983, our family went to the small Grenadian island of Carriacou to help Project Hope and the U.S. Agency for International Development bring medical care to its seven thousand people. One observer characterized the sleepy life on Carriacou as follows: "Very little happens on Carriacou, and what does happen, happens slowly. Hillsborough bustles on Monday, when produce arrives, and on Saturday, mail day. Otherwise, this little town just gazes out to sea."

The clinics were often full, but expectations were low, paperwork was humorously minimal, and complexity was nonexistent. We could perform no laboratory tests, order no X-rays or EKGs, and do no surgery. Yet, surprisingly, as the Carriacouans often observed: "Nothing works, but everything works out."

Although our stay there was a relatively brief six weeks, as a family it was one of the most memorable experiences of our lives. We got up together, ate all our meals together, and often went swimming together. We captured tarantulas together and had crab races on our living room floor together. Perhaps most notably, it was the only time in our parenting when both Linda and I were able to tuck in and pray with our boys every night we were there.

There are few claims the Third World can make of superiority in lifestyle to ours. Having margin, however, is one of them. Third-World living, however, does not assure margin. Missionaries, for example, are sometimes the most exhausted people you'd ever want to meet. Oftentimes the reason these highly motivated people wither under the immense load is not because the developing culture killed their altruism, but rather because they became victims of well-intended self-destruction. Sometimes we take our marginless living with us. When you combine missionary conscientiousness with imported Americanized schedules, and home-office expectations with Third-World need, climate, and disease, burnout is an ever-present risk.

Nobody can keep running on empty. Let's stay busy to be sure. But together let's also develop the necessary theological underpinnings for margin that will allow us to accept its importance without guilt. For just as we need to eat and sleep, so we also need to breathe.

AVAILABILITY

Avid supporters of progress would probably be upset at any suggestion that Third-World cultures have some superior claims to ours. I can hear the rebuttal forming: "What an incredibly regressive idea! If you want to sit on a log all day and watch your children die of disease and your society penalized by ignorance, then go ahead. I'll stick with progress."

But to defend progress and its absence of margin is to presume that all that is good in life and all that God wants us to accomplish is possible only in a booked-up, highly efficient, often exhausted way of life. I do not believe this is true. His asking us to walk the second mile, to carry others' burdens, to witness to the Truth at any opportunity, and to teach our children when we sit, walk, lie, and stand all presuppose we have margin and that we make it available for His purposes. Obedience to these commands is often not schedulable.

Actually, margin is not a spiritual necessity. But availability is. God expects us to be available for the needs of others. And without margin, each of us would have great difficulty guaranteeing availability. Instead, when God calls, He gets the busy signal.

EFFECTS OF NO MARGIN

What would you think if this page had no margins? What would be your opinion of the publishers if they tried to cram the print top to bottom and side to side so that every blank space was filled up? The result would be aesthetically displeasing and chaotic. Like some of our lives.

Yet even if we agree that margin is a good idea, for most of us it seems an unaffordable luxury. We don't really desire to be overdrawn on our personal reserves. It's just that we can't seem to keep it from happening. Overbooking overpowers. There is so much to do and so much to buy. Troublingly, each succeeding year the problem only gets worse.

The effects of no margin are familiar to us all: people who are harried, more concerned with personal sanity than with service to the needs of others; people who have no financial margin, painfully uninterested in hearing of yet another "opportunity" to give. Such people are no longer concerned with building a better world. Instead, they simply want to survive another day. Such people are no longer motivated to meet the needs of others. Instead, they simply want to escape their suffocating schedules. Overworked and overwhelmed victims occupy our no-margined world.

Despite these obvious drawbacks to living without margin, our age consistently deprives us of it. We work hard to gain a foothold of freedom but are quickly pushed back into the quicksand. Overload just happens. Margin, in contrast, requires great effort. Positive margin status is what we call in science an "unstable state," one which spontaneously decays. Margin flows toward overload, but overload does not revert to margin unless forced.

Progress has had many overpriced ideas, but trading us burnout for margin was one of its most uncharitable.

FOUR MARGINS

To be healthy, we require margin in at least four areas: emotional energy, physical energy, time, and finances. Conditions of modern living, however, have drained these margins rather than sustaining them. In emotional energy, seldom have we been so stressed, so alone, and so exhausted in spirit. In physical energy, we are overfed, underactive, and sleep-deprived. In time, our clock-dominated nanosecond culture leaves us wheezing and worn out. And in finances, universal indebtedness makes our societal landscape look like a fiscal Gettysburg.

GROWN ACCUSTOMED TO ITS PACE

My 1982 decision to be involved in medicine only three days a week was not an easy one. I practiced in a wonderful community at a new hospital with an exceptional group of colleagues. My patients respected my judgments and appreciated my care. My income was more than comfortable, and I have never been sued. I had everything a person could desire: a loving family, a prestigious profession, grateful patients, a growing faith, and a life free from need or want. About the only thing I didn't have was margin.

The decision required two years of deliberations and, in the end, was a strongly countercultural thing to do. Yet, when coupled with other lifestyle choices, that decision allowed me the margin I've been writing about. Also, Linda has not worked outside the home since our first child was born.

Of course we didn't simply retire to hammocks but instead dedicated our research to understanding cultural trends, spending thousand of hours in such study. Finally in 1997, I left my University of Wisconsin academic and clinical medical work altogether to further pursue the exploration of cultural medicine and world system problems.

I lived sixteen years without margin: college, medical school, residency, and practice. And, since the decision to cut back my involvement in medicine, I have lived several decades with margin. I can say with certainty that if margin were taken away from me now, I would beg shamelessly to get it back.

MARGIN IN EMOTIONAL ENERGY

OF THE FOUR margins—emotional energy, physical energy, time, and finances—margin in emotional energy is paramount. When we are emotionally resilient, we can confront our problems with a sense of hope and power. When our psychic reserves are depleted, however, we are seriously weakened. Emotional overload saps our strength, paralyzes our resolve, and maximizes our vulnerability, leaving the door open for even further margin erosion.

DEADLINES AND DEAD FRIENDS

Harold was in charge of organizing continuing education for a well-known pharmaceutical firm. He was an excellent communicator. Unfortunately, he was an even better procrastinator. Five months before each conference, Harold's employer required a detailed report of time, events, and speakers, as well as full-text handouts for the topics to be covered.

His boss insisted that the reports be submitted on time—not one day late. Harold, however, never did anything on time. Consequently, three weeks before the approaching deadline, his collapse would begin. Telephones were ringing, printers had questions, secretaries wondered about registration information, computers were spewing out piles of only partially relevant information, and his most important notes were hiding somewhere under a mountain of paper. Harold slept little and argued much. His palms would sweat, but his mouth was dry. He lived on antacids.

Convinced his boss was out to get him, Harold complained, "You can't talk to that man! I hate my work when it gets like this. I don't even like getting up in the morning, let alone going to the office." Nor did it help that he was having trouble in his marriage or that his two teenage daughters were increasingly disrespectful.

"Could you give me something to calm me down?" he asked. "I just can't go on like this."

After our visit, I drew some laboratory tests and gave him a prescription. Later, I called to check how things were going. "Aside from a mildly elevated cholesterol," I said, "your tests all look fine. How are you doing?"

"Much better, Doc. I'm sleeping better now that the deadline has passed. I almost got everything in on time. I'm definitely not as anxious as I was, and I don't feel as depressed."

"How are things at home?" I inquired.

"Better there, too," he said. "Well, that's not exactly true. My daughter's boyfriend shot and killed himself three days ago. So we've had a lot of things to work through. It's been tough on her."

WOUNDS OF THE SPIRIT

When Harold comes in to talk, I hurt with him. I wish I could do more. But there are no quick fixes. His anguish causes me to look progress in the eye and ask, "What's going on here?" Why do so many workers have so much stress? Why do so many marriages have so little vitality? Why do so many adolescents take their own lives? Aren't these fair questions to ask of progress?

Despite the importance of emotional margin, our contemporary level of emotional stamina is not high. Those who predicted the human race would evolve out of emotional problems were mistaken. Such troubles, far from being rarities, rage throughout our society. I am constantly impressed with how drained we seem to be. Broken relationships, financial insecurities, and overburdened schedules rip through us like a chain saw. The wounds we care for in medicine today are more often wounds of the spirit than wounds of the soma.

What happens when our emotional energy reserves are chronically depleted? "If we string ourselves out, expending 100 percent of our time and energy, there is no way in which we can adjust to the unexpected emergency," concludes Pastor Louis H. Evans, Jr. "We become defensive about our expended energies because there isn't anything left to give. Having nothing in reserve, we tune out the need."[1] Stuck in survival mode, there never seems to be enough strength for service.

A Quantum of Emotional Energy

Each morning we rise to meet the day with a certain quantum of emotional energy. For some, this energy reservoir is huge, while for others it is nearly drained empty. Some are buoyant and resilient, filled with a zest and vitality that never seems to change. Others have their emotional chins on the ground and can't remember what it feels like to smile.

This quantum of emotional energy is not fixed but instead is in constant flux with the environment. We are always losing energy into the environment and receiving energy back again. Sometimes the reservoir is being drained, as when we are sad or angry. Other times the reservoir is being filled, perhaps by expressions of encouragement or activities successfully completed.

No matter how large or small the quantum of emotional energy is at the start of the day, and no matter how fast or slow it is exchanging with the environment, one thing is certain: The amount within us is finite. No one has an infinite capacity for emotional discharge. When our reserves are depleted, they are depleted. If we make further withdrawals, pain will be felt.

It is important to understand our emotional reserves. It is important to understand how much we have at the beginning of each day and which influences drain our emotions dry or recharge our batteries. It is important to learn what our limits are, and not to make further withdrawals if we are already maximally depleted. And it is important to respect these limits in others.

We often have trouble accepting the idea of rationing our emotional energy. It is simply too difficult to quantify feelings. We feel ashamed admitting that our spirit is exhausted and collapsing within us. But our hesitancy in no way constitutes proof that such limits are only a convenient fiction for the weak and the lazy. Instead, our hesitancy is an obstacle to overcome. Margin gives us permission.

LIKE WEEDS IN A GARDEN

One would have hoped that the process of progress would have been kind to our emotional life, making it ever easier to replenish our reserves. It might have seemed reasonable to speculate that as our society improved in the areas of education, affluence, and entertainment, we would see a commensurate improvement in overall emotional well-being.

Such has not been the case. These advancements have not resulted in unburdened emotions and liberated psyches. But why not? Our babies seldom die anymore, and famine is virtually unknown to us. We have telephones when we get lonely, air conditioners when we get hot, aspirin when we have a toothache, and television when we get bored. Why then do so many remain so emotionally drained?

I am not suggesting that emotional turmoil and emptiness is an invention of the modern age, for this type of pain has been with us since the beginning of humankind. Yet as our survival needs were secured by civilizational improvements, might we not have expected that emotional disorders would increasingly disappear? Anxiety, depression, suicide and suicide gesturing, personality disorders, obsessive behaviors, eating disorders, panic attacks, alcohol and other drug abuse, phobias, psychoses—these are not diagnoses on the verge of extinction. Instead, these maladies seem to thrive in our society like weeds in a garden. And they all drain us dry emotionally.

Is it possible we are "living in a deteriorating 'psychic environment'"? Over the last several decades, the number of therapists has risen dramatically. According to the National Institute of Health, the burden of mental illness on health and productivity has long been underestimated, and accounts for *over 15 percent of the total "burden of disease" in the US,* ranking second only to ischemic heart disease.[2] Between 22-28 percent of Americans suffer from a mental disorder in any given year.

Many of those trapped in this incredible web of psychic pain are victims, and they are to be commended for seeking help. If you develop typhoid in Bangladesh, it is not the fault of a weak constitution but instead the problem of a highly infectious environment. To seek effective treatment is the appropriate response.

ESCAPING OUR AGE

To our modern era social critics have attached labels that speak of this threatened emotional meltdown. It is not uncommon to hear entire recent decades characterized as the "age of anxiety," the "age of depression," the "age of melancholia," and even the "age of depressed anxiety." The use of tranquilizers has become so prevalent that for decades they have been among the most widely prescribed drugs. All of which prompted one observer to comment, "Millions of suburbanites seem to find that 'the good life' is only endurable under sedation."[3]

When the minor tranquilizers appeared on the scene in 1960, there was great hope. Finally, something to control anxiety and to soothe frazzled nerves! The disillusionment came when we realized that while these drugs did assist in controlling symptoms, they did not cure the underlying problems. People's pain continued, now compounded by tranquilizer addiction.

The widespread use of illicit drugs in our country is evidence that many perceive their personal lot not as a blessing to celebrate but, instead, as a burden to escape from. Why would America's fifteen million problem drinkers risk their bodies, their families, their jobs, and their future for a few hours of drunken stupor? Is it not because they believe the world they enter through alcohol is preferable to the reality they leave behind?

Agent Blue

Norman was a patient in his early sixties, hospitalized the day before. I knew him fairly well, enough to say that we were friends. Yet when I entered his room and approached him with a greeting, he just sat there on the edge of his bed, face drawn, shoulders slumped, looking weakly at his hard-boiled egg.

There was no anger or distance in his silence. I was not offended. I knew that his paralysis came from the malignant darkness of depression. After a minute or so, Norman mumbled in a barely audible voice, "Could you . . . peel my egg? I just . . . can't . . . seem . . ."

The suffering of depression is often unbearable. If you look, you can see it in the eyes: privately tortured eyes reflecting a sea of pain, always misty, ready to overflow at the slightest provocation. When I sit next to such a patient in the examination room, I ask a gently probing question and pass the tissue box at the same time. As the pain surfaces, the tears spill over. It happens 100 percent of the time.

"It is almost impossible to convey to a person who has not had a depression what one is like," explains Jack Dreyfus, founder of the Dreyfus Fund. "It's not obvious like a broken arm, or a fever, or a cough; it's beneath the surface. A depressed person suffers a type of anguish which in its own way can be as painful as anything that can happen to a human being. He has varying degrees of fear throughout the day, and a brain that permits him no rest and races with agitated and frightening thoughts. His mood is low, he has little energy, and he can hardly remember what pleasure means."[4]

Yet in medical practice, depression is a daily finding. It is not limited to a certain socioeconomic group, nor to a certain educational level. No one is immune. Like a flu virus, it strikes any age, any race, any occupation, at any time. Unemployment does heighten the risk, but even successful business executives, such as Jack Dreyfus, suffer from it. High school dropouts might have it, but so do many Harvard graduates. Nihilistic unbelievers feel its pain, but so have some of the greatest preachers in the history of the Church. An increasing number of children and adolescents are being diagnosed with it, and on the other end of the spectrum, many elderly spend their last days caught in its grip.

Researchers are attempting to identify Agent Blue, the unknown factor(s) that causes such a high rate of depression in our society. Despite our impressive advancements in education, affluence, and technology, depression is being diagnosed at higher rates and younger ages. "Adjusting for population growth," explains Gregg Easterbrook, "ten times as many people in the Western nations today suffer from unipolar depression, or unremitting bad feelings, without a specific cause, than did half a century ago. Americans and Europeans have ever more of everything except happiness."[5] This same finding, however, is not occurring in developing countries.

But where is this "dark undertow" coming from? Why, in one morning, were nine of my eleven patients on antidepressants? Where is emotional resilience hiding these days?

CONTEMPORARY LEECHES

The answer lies in the fact that we have been ambushed by psychic pressures unparalleled in human history. This is not to say that other people in other times haven't had it rough. Many have had it much rougher than we do. But never before have people faced the particular constellation of factors that today are plotting together for our misery.

We have already noted how the unprecedented pathogens of stress and overload often wage war on our emotions. Add the assault of speed, the kind whose sheer velocity precludes adaptation to change. Compound the situation by fracturing families, dissipating any sense of community, and decreasing social supports of all kinds. Separate the elderly from their extended families. Add uprootedness by factoring in mobility. Add individualism to narcissism. Alienate adolescents in the direction of R-rated movies, drugs, heavy metal music, early sexuality, and suicide. Add teenage pregnancy and single parenting to welfare dependency. Add child abuse, sexual abuse, and wife abuse to pornography. Add the crime in every city to the reports of crime on every television. Add indebtedness and bankruptcy to job insecurity and demanding bosses. Add unaffordable housing to unaffordable health care. Add traffic to noise to hurry to impossible work schedules to technology that doesn't work to ringing telephones to crying babies.

When you put it all together, there is little wonder we see anxiety and depression. Little wonder the therapists' offices are full. And for each person suffering from a mental or emotional disorder, the lives of at least three other persons are significantly affected.

Restoring Margin in Emotional Energy

If we find our emotional energy gone, how can we get it back? What are the factors that will not only protect our emotional reserves from unnecessary depletion but will replenish the supply at regular intervals? In such a hostile environment, who will be kind to our fragile psyches? Who will feed us and not swallow us?

Following are prescriptions that work; take as needed.

Rx: 1 Cultivate Social Supports

Not only common sense but now also good science, the importance of healthy social supports is irrefutable. We do not simply think they work; we know they work. The mental health slogan "Good Friends Are Good Medicine" is not a cliché; it is state-of-the-art therapeutics.

Whether family and friends or community and church, the existence of intact, functioning, healthy, nurturing systems of social support are as good a resource for replenishing depleted energy reserves as can be found. Love, affection, nurturing, intimacy, connectedness, bonding, attachment, empathy, community—these are "feel good" words for a reason: because they *are* good.

If you find yourself emotionally empty, go to a caring friend. If you are bruised and bleeding, the empathetic response of another will stem the hemorrhage of emotion and begin the process of healing and filling. "There is perhaps no more effective way to relieve psychic pain than to be in contact with another human being who understands what you are going through and can communicate such understanding to you," advises psychiatrist Dr. Frederic Flach.[6]

Not only are verbal expressions of caring important but the physical are as well. Upon entering an exam room, I always made it a practice to shake the hand of my patient or, on occasion, place my hand on his or her shoulder. This, I believe, was the beginning of my therapeutic intervention. We all need human contact. Have you ever noticed how, when a child climbs onto a parent's lap and snuggles in, the entire room feels caressed by the warmth of it?

Rx: 2   Pet a Surrogate

Sometimes, because of social conventions, we are not allowed to touch one another. For those caught in a void and left with a dearth of physical closeness, I would suggest considering surrogates—pets. When God wrote the inviolable law that requires living things to need one another, He included the entire animal world. And it is remarkable how closely we can approximate human-human warmth and affection by substituting human-animal contact. Pets are capable of bonding, are extremely loyal, and often exhibit deep appreciation for our affections—exactly the kind of responses needed to increase our emotional reserves.

Rx: 3   Reconcile Relationships

Broken relationships are a razor across the artery of the spirit. Stemming the hemorrhage and binding the wound should be done as quickly as possible. Yet all too often, it takes months or years. And sometimes, the bleeding never stops.

True reconciliation is one of the most powerful of all human interactions. Warring individuals who have done battle for years can erase all antagonism in a matter of minutes. This is not a matter of human psychology but rather a divine gift. One of the great privileges of our adoption into God's family is the access we have to this mysterious healing power of the Spirit. If you have not seen it happen, or if you have only seen it happen rarely, then yearn for it. Pray for it. Beg for it. And know that it is one of the gifts God most enjoys giving.

Rx: 4   Serve One Another

Medical studies reveal that service is health enhancing. One of the best ways to heal your own emotional pain is to focus instead on meeting the needs of others. It works, powerfully. Perhaps it is God closing his own feedback loop.

"We must be purposely kind and generous, or we miss the best part of existence," observed Horace Mann. "The heart that goes out of itself gets large and full of joy. This is the great secret of the inner life. We do ourselves the most good doing something for others." The service can be noble and sacrificial, or it can be small and simple. Not to worry, explains Rudyard Kipling, "for the glory of the Garden glorifieth everyone."

A University of Michigan study followed 2,700 people for over a decade to see how their social relationships affected their health and well-being. Those who performed regular volunteer work showed dramatically increased life expectancy. Men not involved in such altruistic activity had two-and-one-half times the morbidity during the period studied than those who volunteered at least once a week.

In the 1980s, a 110-mile-per-hour windstorm blasted across our county, leveling trees, power lines, and buildings, and causing $60 million in damage. Within days, people from several eastern states began quietly arriving in town, volunteers of the Mennonite Disaster Service. Some stayed as long as a month, living in university dormitories vacated for the summer. Most were involved in the rebuilding of barns. I don't remember what I did those weeks after the storm, but I will never forget what they did. They served. Every time I think of the disaster, I think also of the gift. Do you see the multiplying effects of this virtue?

I recently heard of a man who, while driving on the interstate highway system, pays not only his own toll but also the toll for the car to follow. In so doing, he is making deposits in at least three emotional bank accounts: his own, the teller's, and the following driver's.

My wife, Linda, is always alert to ways of serving others. Stopping at a convenience store recently for some ice cream, she happened to mention at the counter that it was for cherry pie. "Sounds great!" responded the youthful clerk. Fifteen minutes later, Linda brought him a huge piece of fresh cherry pie à la mode. That evening, alone in the store, he was nourished by service. A simple thing; a magnificent obsession.

And the gift goes on . . .

Rx: 5 Rest

Be with people and serve them. But be sure to get away occasionally. Escape. Relax. Sleep in. Take a nap. Unplug the phone and turn off the beeper. Try setting aside time regularly for some quiet and for rest.

Many of us funnel all our rest needs into already jam-packed weekends and holidays. But don't fall into the trap of thinking weekends and holidays are restful. Often they are not. Sometimes they are even more draining than the week we just escaped. Weekends, Sundays, holidays, vacations—all have been modernized, and are only restful if forced to behave.

When emotionally exhausted, the first thing I do is find quiet, solitude, and a chance to do nothing. I don't feel guilty, for fallow times are just as important as productive times. I cycle quickly, and my energy will return shortly. All I need is quiet and some time.

Even Jesus did the same: "The apostles gathered around Jesus and reported to him all they had done and taught. Then, because so many people were coming and going that they did not even have a chance to eat, he said to them, 'Come with me by yourselves to a quiet place and get some rest.' So they went away by themselves in a boat to a solitary place."[7]

Rest restores.

Rx: 6 Laugh

People who laugh readily heal faster. Medical authorities are still trying to figure out exactly how this works physiologically. But clearly, humor is medicinal. It tastes better than pills, it works as well, and it costs less. Why do you think children are so buoyant, so resilient, so capable of picking themselves up and going on? Among the many reasons, laughter is prominent.

By the time babies are four months old, they already are laughing once every hour. And by the age of four years, these clowns laugh on average once every four minutes—or four hundred times a day. By the time we reach adulthood, however, we manage only fifteen laughs a day.

Try laughing every four minutes. I guarantee something positive will happen to your emotions. One psychiatrist recommends a half-hour of therapeutic laughter every day.

Perhaps the best kind of laughter is when we laugh at ourselves—we never run out of material. After Hurricane Andrew leveled his house, a man in south Florida put out a sign reading: "Open house." He will heal faster than his neighbors.

New studies indicate that even the anticipation of a humorous event— as far as two days in advance—will begin reducing stress hormone levels and boosting the immune system.[8]

Laughter doesn't require a Ph.D. degree or a six-figure salary. It is a free God-given gift. Perhaps He knew we would need it.

Rx: 7   Cry

Sometimes we laugh so hard we cry. Other times we just cry. Crying is a form of emotional purging. As long as it is not an indication of a deeper depression (in which case frequent weeping is a symptom that should not be ignored), crying can have salutary health benefits. According to some studies, those who cry *more often* get sick *less often*. A good cry usually lasts six or seven minutes and releases a burdensome load of emotional pollution.

Laughter lifts; crying cleanses. Both are partners in the process of emotional restoration.

Rx: 8   Create Appropriate Boundaries

Boundaries are about establishing a perimeter around the personal and private spaces of our lives and not letting the world come crashing in uninvited. This is not an issue of selfishness but instead of self-care.

In our home, for example, we have the boundary of not answering the telephone during dinner hour. We're not trying to be rude and we hope they will call back. But whatever is happening around the table is more important than whoever is calling. After all, a people have the right to establish and defend the atmosphere of their own home.

The need to establish boundaries is a mathematical necessity. With far too many demands and expectations upon us, we could not possibly fulfill them all even should we desire to do so. We, then, must respond with grace, with sensitivity, yet with firmness: "I'm sorry, but I can't." To be able to say no without guilt is to be freed from one of the biggest monsters in our overburdened lives. If we decline, not out of self-serving laziness but for God-honoring balance and health, then this level of control will not only protect our emotional margin but will actually increase it.

"Boundary deficits," explains psychologist Dr. John Townsend, "can be deeply disabling to anyone, including Christians. People with unclear boundaries can find themselves making commitments under pressure that they would never make with a clear head. They find themselves 'caving in' to others. We need to find maturing, caring people who will love our boundaries just as much as they love our attachment. . . . Ask yourself, 'Do the people closest to me love my *no* as much as they love my *yes*?'"[9]

Rx: 9   *Envision a Better Future*

Each of us must have a transcendent vision: a hopeful, spiritually valid expectation of what the future will hold. We all must have a purpose bigger than ourselves that we can live for. We must have something we can believe in, something we can give ourselves to. A transcendent vision with purpose, meaning, direction, and structure.

Unfortunately, there has been a wholesale destruction of vision in modern-day living. Aimlessness is like a metaphysical black hole, swallowing up everything in sight. Perhaps the most poignant description of our existential emptiness comes from the French philosopher Jean-Paul Sartre, when he speaks of "man as a bubble of consciousness in an ocean of nothingness, bobbing around until the bubble pops."[10]

So here we have a clear choice: the vision and spirit of the age—which is really a vote for despair followed by death—or the vision of the revealed Word of God. If we believe in and work for something larger than ourselves—for our families, for the community, for the common good, and for the kingdom—then every expenditure of emotion will have meaning, and every expenditure of emotion will be reimbursable.

Rx: 10 *Offer Thanks*

In everyone's life there is much to be grateful for and also much to be unhappy about. Realistically acknowledging both ends of the spectrum is appropriate. Unfortunately, most of the time our emotions dwell on our problems and forget about our obligation to gratitude.

If you were handed a 3 x 5 card and asked to write on it one thing you are grateful for, and then another card and another card . . . How many cards would it take before you ran out of reasons to be thankful? I hope 10,000.

If we will pull our minds and our spirits away from our problems from time to time and redirect them to our blessings, we will find much to celebrate. We'll recognize that the world is full of beauty, that most people are worthy of our respect and trust, and that the affairs of suffering humans are replete with acts of love, kindness, nobility, and sacrifice. And we'll remember that overseeing it all is a God who knows us well, who loves us anyway, and who is very, very good.

All people have within their grasp much to be thankful for. Gratitude fills. Grumbling drains. The choice is ours.

Rx: 11 *Grant Grace*

I don't think most of us realize what a weighty emotional burden it is to judge others and to be judged in return. It is a form of emotional and spiritual suicide—like chopping a hole in the bottom of your lifeboat because you don't want the other person to be rescued.

Grace, on the other hand, treats people not as they deserve but better than they deserve. Grace preempts accusation, freeing both parties. When we extend grace to our enemies, they receive a shockingly unexpected glimpse of the kingdom. And, at precisely the same time that our adversary is released, we are as well.

Why would anyone wish to go around carrying a donkey on his shoulders when he could ride instead? Why would anyone wish to be harsh when he could instead be free? "If thou knewest all the Bible . . . and also the sayings of all philosophers by heart," asks Thomas à Kempis, "what should it profit thee without grace and charity?"[11]

Grace not only revives emotional margin, it lifts it to heaven.

Rx: 12 Be Rich in Faith

"And now these three remain: *faith*, hope and love."[12]

"Seeing isn't believing," once quipped George MacDonald. "It's only seeing."

Faith, however, is seeing without seeing. The faith of our fathers that successfully withstood dungeon, fire, and sword is the same faith that leads us safely through contemporary dangers, toils, and snares. If it can withstand anything, then can it not withstand the problems of modernity? To be sure, when all hammers are dust, the anvil will yet endure. Even when all else fails us, year after year, faith remains. In his book *Resilience*, psychiatrist Dr. Friedrich Flach states, "I believe the most vital ingredient of resilience is faith."[13]

Rx: 13 Hold Fast Hope

"And now these three remain: faith, *hope* and love."

The world does not have a strong articulation of the concept of hope, nor does it have a credible basis for developing one. "The *Encyclopedia Britannica* has columns on love and faith, but not a single word about hope," observed the late psychiatrist Dr. Karl Menninger.[14] Despite this conspicuous textual absence, explains Harvard psychiatrist Dr. Armand Nicholi, "Psychiatrists have long suspected that hope fosters health, both physical and emotional." With the need for hope established, where in a despairing world do we find it? "When we turn to the New Testament," says Dr. Nicholi, "we read again and again: 'Christ Jesus, our hope.'"[15]

Although acknowledging that "the optimism of inevitable progress has become tarnished," Princeton philosopher and theologian Diogenes Allen sees great cause for hope. "The kingdom of God is at hand when it becomes harder and harder to ignore or evade God's ways. Such convictions enable Christians to continue to work for the common good, to be philanthropic, even in a deteriorating situation. Because of faith in the good God intends us to have, Christian hope can survive even the disintegration of a culture."[16]

Scripture reminds us of the hope of the promise, the hope of the gospel, and the hope of salvation. The apostle Paul writes, "And we rejoice in the hope of the glory of God. Not only so, but we also rejoice in our sufferings, because we know that suffering produces perseverance; perseverance, character; and character, hope. And hope does not disappoint us, because God has poured out his love."[17]

Rx: 14 *Above All, Love*

"And now these three remain: faith, hope and *love*."

To have accepted the love of God is to be armed and disarmed at the same time. No weapon is more powerful. But in using such a weapon it is the user who is broken wide open. This is a love that cannot rightly be kept in—it is a bursting-out love. In its spilling out, it binds to others. And when it binds to others, it heals, it knits hearts, it builds community, and it brings everything "together in perfect unity."[18] "The effort to 'love thy neighbor as thyself' probably has done more good, and more to make life pleasant, than any other guideline," observes Dr. Selye.[19]

Love is the only medicine I know of which, when used according to directions, heals completely yet takes one's life away. It is dangerous; it is uncontrollable; it is "self-expenditure"; and it can never be taken on any terms but its own. Yet as a healer of the emotions, it has no equal.

"But the greatest of these is love."[20]

8

MARGIN IN PHYSICAL ENERGY

WHEN WE DIP into the tank for some physical energy, we all want the ladle to return with something in it. Unfortunately, for too many of us the tank dried up years ago.

A large percentage of Americans are sadly out of shape and have diminished physical energy reserves because of poor conditioning. Others, such as mothers of newborns and those who work two jobs, are chronically sleep-deprived. Still others suffer from chronic biscuit poisoning. These three factors — poor conditioning, sleep deprivation, and obesity — constitute a physical energy desert where no margin can grow.

Lacking margin in physical energy, we feel underrested and overwhelmed. With no strength left for our own needs, let alone the needs of others, we put our tiredness to bed hoping tomorrow will be a stronger day.

THE NEW MORBIDITY

Thanks to progress, extraordinary tools are available to assist us in living healthier, longer lives. Once again, however, we unexpectedly find a dark side to it all. Gone are the old infectious foes, but replacing them are a variety of frustrating enemies variously known as "the new morbidity," "the diseases of civilization," and "the diseases of lifestyle." These ailments come as a result of our bad habits and poor choices. Medical authorities repeatedly bemoan a national "epidemic of poor health practices," and estimate that more than 50 percent of all deaths are related to lifestyle choices.

The prevalence of lifestyle-related pathologies certainly makes medicine a secure profession. Those who predicted the human race would evolve into a communal picture of nontoxic, robust heartiness have been deeply shaken by the statistics of the last few decades. Not only are health professionals still needed, but even with the addition of alternative health practitioners, we are all still working overtime. Progress brings technology, affluence, and education, but not the kind of inner discipline necessary to maintain sound physical health.

In some ways, progress is too easy on us. It provides electricity and artificial lighting, but without regard for the requirement of sleep. It caters food in overabundance, but without regard for the requirement of restraint. And it supplies transportation and convenience, but without regard for the requirement of physical activity. As a result, we sleep too little, eat too much, and move hardly at all.

PERCHANCE TO SLEEP

We live in "drowsy America," where factories, grocery stores, service stations, and restaurants are open through the night. Cultural and economic forces have turned the U.S. into a 24-hour society. As a result, the average American today gets two and one-half hours less sleep *per night* than 100 years ago.

Many round-the-clock cities never go to sleep. Students pull "all-nighters" studying for exams; nurses check on sleeping patients and watch the monitors; taxi drivers listen to an all-night station on their radios and drive denizens of the dark around town. Mothers of young children work all day in the office and then all night in the nursery. Shift workers—a growing percentage of the labor force—miss more days of work, use more caffeine, suffer more drug abuse, and take more sleep medication than the average American. Only 15 percent of teens get the minimum recommended 8.5 hours of sleep they need per night, and this sleep deficit is additionally linked to other problems such as obesity, attention deficit symptoms, and depression. Sleep deprivation has become one of the most pervasive health problems facing the U.S.

BEST-SELLING ADIPOSE

Each new series of reports contain the same two messages: We're a heavy people, and it's always getting worse. Of course there are many good reasons for this: We have an abundant supply of safe, inexpensive food; we have the affluence to buy as much as we desire; and it all tastes fabulous.

Obesity, or the "rounding of America," is such a ubiquitous problem that one-fourth to one-half of all adults are on a diet at any given time. The list of best sellers always has several dieting books. Fifty-five percent of American adults are either overweight or obese. The incidence of childhood obesity is up alarmingly. And many obesity-related diseases, such as Type II diabetes, are also rising. As John Kenneth Galbraith once observed: "More die in the United States of too much food than of too little."

EXTINCT EXERCISE

Some think the cause of our adipose problem is not that we eat too much, but we move too little. Our prosperity has allowed us to be cerebral and sedentary rather than physically robust, and lack of exercise has brought problems beyond obesity. In earlier eras, the sheer harshness of existence required a physically active lifestyle. During Revolutionary War days, when 90 percent of our population were farmers, physical labor was an indispensable part of daily activity. Today, however, only 2 percent of Americans earn their living off the land. The rest of us sit behind desks and push pencils rather than pitching hay bales. And, as we sit, we thicken.

Restoring Margin in Physical Energy

Our bodies are, in one sense, sophisticated energy machines. If we properly care for the engine and load the appropriate fuel, our machine will operate reliably. Even when called upon to double or triple its performance, the body is capable of responding by tapping into energy reserves.

These reserves can be enhanced or depleted depending upon many factors—some external, some internal, and some eternal. It is wise for us to vigilantly protect these reserves, for if they are drawn too low, ill results follow. We are left not only exhausted but unprotected as well.

Virtually anyone, however, no matter how ravaged by insomnia, intemperance, and inactivity, can take steps to improve these reserves. The rules for restoring energy to the human body are not written out in calculus and hidden in the catacombs. On the contrary, they are a matter of public record, accessible to all.

The body can bounce back; God designed it so. But not without some cooperation from its owner. "Healing is a matter of time," said Hippocrates, "but it is sometimes also a matter of opportunity." Let's look together at some prescriptions that might help.

Rx: 1   Take Personal Responsibility

I learned long ago that I can inform but not perform that which is needed in the lives of my patients. Until we accept personal responsibility for our own health, the road to the future will remain paved with aches and adipose.

If you are underslept, overweight, and unexercised, it is your job to change. I want to encourage you that change is possible. But just as the body is yours, so is the responsibility.

Rx: 2   Gain Physical Margin Through Emotional Margin

In this chapter we will concentrate on the physical components of restoring energy. Never slight, however, the role that emotions play in our quest. A natural, God-ordained mutuality exists between physical and emotional well-being. We have seen how social supports, nurturing relationships, service, volunteerism, laughter, purpose, vision, gratitude, grace, faith, hope, and love are all important to emotional health. They are equally important to physical health.

I encourage seekers of physical energy to look beyond the diet and exercise books and to first seek enhanced physical vitality through enhanced emotional vitality.

Rx: 3   Change Your Habits

Poor nutrition, poor exercise patterns, and (sometimes) poor sleep hygiene are called "habit disorders." Breaking old ways and establishing new patterns are necessary.

Changing habit disorders often requires changing lifestyles. Sometimes the changes required are small. More often, however, the adjustment entails a new way of looking at and reacting to both yourself and the world around you. In making these changes, it helps to surround yourself with a subculture of people who will support the changes rather than undermine them.

THE RITES OF SLEEP

Rx: 4   Value of Sleep

Many people have negative attitudes toward sleep. Often these are very productive people who resent the "wasted time." They also tend to be people who need less than average sleep themselves. Unfortunately, this attitude too often forces its way into other bedrooms uninvited.

Don't get caught in a web of shame spun by other people. A good night's sleep is not an embarrassment. It's not necessary to feel guilty if you are well rested. Sleep was God's idea. He created the necessity, and "he grants sleep to those he loves."[1] The need for sleep is undeniable and should be regarded as an ally, not an enemy. To sleep soundly for a full night is a valuable restorative gift. As anyone who has read Proverbs knows, however, the sluggard is left defenseless by Scripture.

Choose to get enough rest. Determine how much sleep you need to feel your best and then determine to get it. I personally feel best with seven to eight hours of sleep, as do the majority of adults.

Rx: 5   Develop Healthy Sleep Patterns

Many people don't sleep well simply because they practice poor sleep habits. Develop a healthy pattern of sleep. Retire at a similar time each evening; arise at a similar time each morning. Have a quiet room and a good mattress. If you suffer from cold feet, prewarm the sheets with an electric blanket. Don't engage in disturbing conversations immediately before bedtime. Instead, begin relaxing about an hour or so before retiring. Give yourself time to unwind from the day. Don't have a big meal within two hours of bedtime. Limit the intake of caffeine in the evening and, if necessary, in the afternoon as well. If you are a clock watcher, turn the clock toward the wall.

If sleep is delayed by racing thoughts or creativity, keep a notebook or even a small tape recorder next to the bed. Frequently I will scribble myself notes in the dark and then set the paper on the floor where I will see it first thing in the morning. My mind thus emptied is free to sleep.

Rx: 6   Don't Catastrophize Insomnia

"The best cure for insomnia," said W. C. Fields, "is to get enough sleep." If only . . .

When insomnia strikes, don't panic. It happens to everybody from time to time, and one or two nights of sleeplessness do not constitute a crisis. What can become a crisis, however, is your reaction.

After one or two nights of sleeplessness, a pattern develops. Annoyance turns to fear, then fear turns to panic. And nothing retards sleep like panic. Trying to force yourself to sleep is the surest way of preventing somnolence. "Sleep is one of the few things in life that cannot be improved upon by trying harder," explains sleep expert Dr. Peter Hauri.

If insomnia is a problem, don't stay in bed awake. Get up, sit in a comfortable chair or lie on the couch, read, write a letter, have a light snack, drink some milk, take a walk, soak in the bathtub, play relaxing music, watch television. But don't worry.

Consider turning the night into a conversation with God. Pray. Listen. Meditate. Read the Word. Begin a spiritual journal. Listen to soothing radio. And don't forget to thank Him for the special opportunity of this time together. When tiredness begins to overtake you, retire once again.

Insomnia can sometimes be a symptom of depression. Instead of poor initiation of sleep, however, the sleeplessness of depression is usually characterized by early awakening. For this condition, antidepressant medications can often be very helpful. They are not sleeping pills—although they can have a beneficial sedative side effect. They are not narcotics—although some can help greatly with chronic pain and its associated sleeplessness. And they are not addicting.

Although there are occasional indications for sleeping pills, it's not a good idea to depend on them. If you are undergoing a particularly stressful event in your life, sometimes a sleeping aid for a few days will keep sleepless exhaustion from compounding your troubles. But don't use them for more than two weeks.

Rx: 7   Don't Oversleep

As a rule, oversleeping will make you feel worse rather than better. Extra sleeping paradoxically often causes extra tiredness. Also, headaches are more common with excess sleep.

Rx: 8   Take a Nap

Every function of the human body undergoes a diurnal variation, meaning that it fluctuates and phases throughout the day. In the early afternoon, for example, our body experiences a physiologic slump resulting in a mild natural sleepiness.

Many of the world's greatest leaders were nappers. Thomas Edison is said to have catnapped up to eight times a day. John F. Kennedy napped in the White House, and Churchill took daily naps during World War II. Even Jesus napped.

Naps can be revitalizing. If you have the opportunity and need to nap, it is best to follow certain guidelines. If you nap for longer than one hour, understand that a longer nap is not necessarily more restful. The most helpful and natural naps are in the afternoon, but a short nap in the early evening can give added stamina for the hours ahead. A longer evening nap, however, will often hinder the initiation of sleep that night.

Rx: 9   Exercise for Sounder Sleep

One of the first benefits people notice when they embark on an exercise program is sounder sleep. Healthy physical tiredness probably has no equal as a sleep-inducing sedative. Don't, however, exercise vigorously just before going to bed, as muscle discomfort can retard the initiation of sleep.

THE RECIPES OF NUTRITION

Rx: 10   Decrease Intake of Fat, Sugars, and Total Calories

Dietary and nutritional advice has been changing rapidly in recent years, and I am not inclined to stake out a dogmatic position until the debate has quieted. However, in general, it is always wise to decrease total caloric intake. No matter which diet you follow, calories still count. Because fat is calorie dense (having twice as many calories per pound as carbohydrates or protein), it is wise to restrain fat consumption. Carbohydrates are another major culprit, particularly simple carbohydrates such as sugar. The average American now eats approximately 150 pounds of sugar a year, mostly in the form of "hidden" sugar added during food processing.

Of course, we all know we should eat fewer calories, but we eat more anyway. There are three main reasons for this: It all tastes good, it is our habit, and we can afford to. In rebuttal: There are healthier foods that also taste good, we can change our bad habits, and we can't afford not to.

Rx: 11   Replace Processed Snacks with Fruit

Fruits can be a good substitute for fats and "hidden" sugars. Oftentimes we bypass fruits thinking they are too expensive. Then we travel down the aisle and pick out cookies, chips, and candy instead. If you do the math, however, you will discover that by weight, fruit is almost always cheaper than processed snacks . . . and far healthier.

Rx: 12 Avoid Overeating

Put smaller portions on the table. Use a smaller plate. Chew food longer. Set your fork down between every bite. Don't prepare the next bite until you have finished chewing and swallowing the one in your mouth. Consciously taste your food. Don't take seconds. Always sit down to eat. Eat at only one place in the house. Don't eat in front of the television. Don't snack. Bite your tongue.

Rx: 13 Garden or Buy Direct

There are two ways to process food: God's way and the factory way. God has our best interest at heart; the factories sometimes don't. The ground, taking its orders from God, fortunately doesn't process food the way factories do. And, generally speaking, the less factory processing, the better the food. Always protect the most direct connection from the Father's hand to your table. Without getting into an extensive discussion about chemicals and additives, suffice it to say that my main concern is the added salt, sugar, and calories found in factory-processed foods. Avoid them if you can.

Rx: 14 Drink a Lot of Water

The universal recommendation is six to eight glasses of water a day. For many, ice water is more palatable than tap water. Drinking a large glass of water before sitting down for a meal can help keep you full and suppress the appetite.

Rx: 15 Use Exercise as Both Appetite and Weight Reducer

It is a myth that exercise increases appetite. In most cases, vigorous exercise diminishes appetite, sometimes even to the point of nausea. So if it works for you, sweat before you eat.

Also, if the goal is weight reduction, combine exercise with dieting. Dieting alone will result in the loss of not only fat but also lean body tissue such as muscle. On the other hand, exercise alone requires a huge amount of effort for a small amount of weight loss.

Every extra pound we gain equals 3,500 calories. For a 150 pound person, burning this number of calories would require 20 hours of slow walking,

10 hours of vigorous walking, or 4 hours of swimming. Obviously, relying on exercise alone for weight reduction will yield frustratingly meager results. The sensible approach combines both calorie restriction and calorie incineration in a weight-reduction program.

Rx: 16 McStay at Home

Americans now spend over $1 billion a day eating out, usually choosing higher caloric foods than when eating at home. For some, the difference between normal weight and obesity is the simple difference between eating in and eating out.

THE REGIMENS OF EXERCISE

Rx: 17 Exercise for the Heart

There are five aspects to a fitness evaluation: cardiorespiratory endurance, muscle strength, muscle endurance, flexibility, and body composition. Of these, the most important and beneficial is cardiorespiratory endurance.

Think of your heart as a plow horse. You abuse it and abuse it—but it never complains. And then one day in the middle of a furrow, it drops dead.

Don't abuse your heart. It is your workhorse. Every day it beats one hundred thousand times and pumps sixteen hundred gallons of blood over sixty thousand miles of vessels. Say thank you to your heart. Buy it roses. Encourage it every chance you get.

One way you can encourage your heart is by conditioning it. Through exercise, for example, you could cut your heart rate from perhaps eighty beats a minute down to sixty. In so doing, you would save your heart over ten million beats a year. As a token of its appreciation, it would send you back a gift. Try it for a few months and see what the gift is.

A specific fitness program aimed at conditioning the cardiorespiratory system focuses on the body's ability to deliver and use oxygen. Aerobic conditioning trains your heart, your lungs, your blood, and your blood vessels in such a way that they can deliver more oxygen faster and more efficiently to the body. This is accomplished by performing thirty to forty-five minutes of sustained exercise—walking, jogging, swimming, bicycling, etc.—three or four times a week.

A common misconception people have is that they already live an active life, so why all the fuss? They are on their feet all day, up and down stairs, lifting, bending, stooping, and generally on the go continuously. They always come home tired; therefore, they assume they get plenty of exercise. It is important to recognize, however, that although this might be a busy lifestyle in one sense, it is not conditioning exercise.

Rx: 18 Exercise for the Muscles

A second kind of exercise has to do with skeletal muscle development. While weight lifting and calisthenics do not constitute overall aerobic conditioning, they can give enhanced strength, speed, agility, and self-esteem.

There are two aspects to muscle fitness—strength and endurance. In a weight-training program, lifting heavier weights with fewer repetitions increases strength, while lifting lighter weights with more repetitions increases endurance. As we age, muscle strength declines more quickly than does muscle endurance.

I do not support weight training for the vanity of it. But neither should it be forsaken simply because it is misused by bronzed bodies who flaunt it. The simple fact is, progress wrongly released us from the need to use our muscles, and if we do not use them we lose them.

Rx: 19 Exercise for Flexibility

Flexibility exercising is the least demanding in terms of wear and tear. We seldom huff, puff, or sweat. Yet it can help keep us moving and decrease our aches and pains, particularly in the neck, shoulders, and low back.

As we age, our flexibility becomes constricted. Watch the contortions of young children and compare them to your own creaky hinges. Undergoing a program of flexibility can help regain some of the lost range of motion with laudatory results.

Rx: 20 *Exercise for the Mind and Spirit*

One hundred percent of people who exercise to the point of cardiorespiratory fitness will experience an increased sense of well-being. Exercise has a tranquilizing effect on the body. It helps decompress stress and is good medicine for anxiety or depression. Along with increased energy, it grants increased alertness, independence, dignity, self-esteem, and sleep. "Exercise isn't just for the physically unfit. It's for the mentally unfit, too. I can recommend it for anyone who's depressed," explains aerobic expert Kenneth Cooper, M.D. "If exercise benefits the body, it can do wonders for the mind."[2]

Rx: 21 *Bike or Walk*

When studying in Switzerland for a year, I lived with a Swiss family. My "Swiss father," a physician-researcher, rode his bicycle to and from work each day, including a round trip home for lunch. My Swiss mother walked to town each morning to buy groceries for the day—bread, vegetables, meat, milk. They were not alone in these habits. As I daily made my way to the study center, the streets would be crowded with bicyclists and pedestrians.

As citizens of the most prosperous country in the world, the Swiss could afford to drive, but chose not to. Although the pattern has shifted over the years to more automobile use, I will never forget the example of health that was set for me that year.

In the United States, however, we go everywhere in our cars. Vehicles have become easy chairs on wheels. And when we arrive at our destinations, we don't even disembark. Instead, we "drive up" for our banking and "drive through" for our fast food. I've even heard of a drive-up church and a drive-up baby clinic where you lift your child through the window to a waiting pediatrician.

Instead, park the car a block from your destination. Get off the bus or subway one stop early. Climb stairs rather than use the elevator. Any exercise is better than no exercise, even if it is a walk of only ten steps.

Rx: 22 *Choose What Works for You*

Find the kind of exercise that is most practical and enjoyable for you. "The generic drug here is exercise, and running is simply a brand," explains fitness activist George Sheehan, M.D. "It's a question of finding your brand of the drug."

Don't start playing racquetball if you hate the sport. I don't enjoy swimming and get cold every time I enter the water. So if I decided to swim as my exercise, I would be guaranteeing failure. Currently, my favorite activity is yard work—mowing the lawn, working in the garden, cutting trees and wood for our wood burner, cleaning brush. Walking is perhaps the most universal choice: it is readily accessible, it is not strenuous, it can be done with a friend or pet, it requires no specific equipment or preparation, and it can be done in nearly all weather conditions.

Rx: 23 Stick with It

You will be able to find many temptations to quit any exercise program. Many complain of being too tired. But when you feel too tired to exercise is actually a good time to do it. Often, paradoxically, you will feel less tired after the workout than before.

Have you ever noticed how you can come home fatigued, only to see the exhaustion disappear soon thereafter when doing something enjoyable? I remember one evening being very tired but needing to mow the lawn anyway (something I normally enjoy doing). After fifteen minutes, I was surprised to notice that my tiredness had disappeared. Fatigue often has its source in emotional rather than muscular or cardiovascular exhaustion.

Another reason people quit exercising is discouragement, the feeling that all this effort isn't doing any good. What you don't realize is that it *is* doing good—you just can't fully sense it yet. Approach exercise as an investment. If you don't begin to receive dividends within two months, you have my permission to quit.

Rx: 24 Be Realistic

One of my patients with advanced lung cancer came in wearing a concerned look. "Doctor, I had my cholesterol tested and it is 221. Is that too high?" Her death three months later had nothing to do with cholesterol. There are enough problems to worry about without adding nonproblems to the list.

- Focus on the important issues. If you are forty pounds overweight, don't worry about how much vitamin C is in a potato.
- Choose appropriate exercises. If you are elderly, it is probably best not to choose a running program. If you have arthritis or chronic low back pain, you may need to choose nonweightbearing exercises such as swimming or cycling (although a walking program is often beneficial for low back pain).
- If dieting, aim to lose only one to two pounds a week. Don't try to climb twenty stairs in a single bound. Slow changes are more sustainable.
- Be patient and persistent. "How poor are they who have no patience!" wrote William Shakespeare. "What wound did ever heal but by degrees?"
- Fads, scams, and frauds have a therapeutic value "as thin as the homeopathic soup that was made by boiling the shadow of a pigeon that had been starved to death," to borrow from Abraham Lincoln. Remember, all diets work short-term. Invest in fact-based regimens with proven long-term benefits.
- Expect to have ups and downs. Even the experts do.
- Set goals, but let them be reachable.
- Believe in yourself. I do.

The body is a miracle of complexity and sophistication that exceeds comprehension. Fortunately, most of it runs on automatic pilot—the heart beats, the blood circulates, the glands secrete, the enzymes catalyze, the electrolytes balance, the glucose metabolizes, the liver detoxifies. Even our thinking and breathing are largely automatic and involuntary; our brain and lungs function not because we tell them to but because God tells them to.

God gave us an amazing gift, and all we are required to do is feed it, water it, rest it, and move it. Yet it needs to be the right food, water, rest, and movement.

If we perform our assignment well, we will find energy we never knew we had. We will work better, run better, feel better, heal better, and live better.

CHAPTER 9

MARGIN IN TIME

TED ANDERSON ROSE at 5:00 AM to howling winds and drifting snow. He washed, pulled on his work clothes, and headed for the barn. Familiar with work he enjoys, Ted started feeding the 150 head of Angus cattle and attending to his other farm chores. By 7:00 AM, he was back inside to have breakfast with his wife, Jae, and help get three-year-old Lottie Marie ready for the day. Quickly changing clothes, his next challenge on this frigid morning was to survive the icy roads into St. Paul. The usual one-hour commute to his systems-analyst job always takes longer when detoured through Siberia.

Meanwhile, Jae and Lottie Marie set off on an icy Wisconsin adventure of their own, braking and sliding the fifteen minutes to the veterinarian clinic where Jae is a full-time technician and animal groomer. Lottie has done well spending her first three years in the clinic. As a baby, she would sit in an infant seat or lie on a blanket. Now that she is older, she is always easily entertained. Each afternoon she takes a long nap in the back room.

After Ted returned home at 7:00 PM, he finished the remaining chores on their eighty-acre farm. Most evenings, this was an hour or two of work.

Besides their own farm, the Andersons rent an additional eight hundred acres for open pasturing and for raising hay, corn, and oats. These crops have to be planted, cultivated, fertilized, harvested, baled, chopped, and stored. And, of course, the farm equipment has to be cleaned and maintained as well.

Anyone who would accept the job of vaccinating 150 head of cattle must be familiar with animals, and Jae is. She also has additional dogs, sheep, and horses of her own to care for.

Obviously, the Andersons are a hard-working young family. They love animals, farming, rural living, and challenges. But they are marginless.

"What would happen if Lottie got sick?" I asked.

"She never has. We've been fortunate."

"Do you breed your herd?" I asked. "What happens during calving? How do you manage to monitor the births?"

"The Angus is famous for easy calving," explained Jae. "It usually just happens. All we do is check every day before and after work. Oftentimes we discover a calf that has already been born—or three or four. Then we take any newborns, weigh them, tag and vaccinate them, and give them back to mom. If any trouble arises, we have someone from the vet clinic come and help."

Lately, however, the system has been tested. This spring, the crops were planted late. Bad weather this fall delayed their harvest. The corn is now in storage, but wet with snow.

A few months ago, some heifers were frightened out of the pasture by hunters. After the neighbors called, the chase was on. "We had to get help," explained Jae. "One person can't just run out and catch a nine-hundred-pound black heifer in the middle of the night without help." Some mischievous heifers continued to elude capture. Two were hit by cars on the road, necessitating police involvement.

Deciding to artificially inseminate one hundred cows this summer was a further strain. This type of breeding requires observing the herd closely. For several hours each morning and again each evening, the cows must be walked into a corral and watched. If any are in heat, they have to be separated out for insemination. This demand saw other chores suffer.

Since making the decision to expand their own family, Ted and Jae are planning some changes in their workload. "We are going to sell off at least half the cows and rent a smaller acreage next year," Jae explained. "And after the second baby is born, I will be quitting my job."

"How do you feel about that?" I inquired.

"Wonderful!" she explained through her fever and flu. "I love my job, and my boss is a good friend. But it will be wonderful to have more time at home."

TIME AND HOW WE TALK

Ted and Jae, along with millions of other Americans, live busy lives. Their industry and fortitude are reminiscent of the pioneer spirit that carved a great nation out of a huge wilderness. They have work, a family, and a farm—all of which they enjoy. About the only thing they don't have is margin.

"I love a broad margin to my life," posited another farmer (of sorts), Henry David Thoreau. "Sometimes, in a summer morning, having taken my accustomed bath, I sat in my sunny doorway from sunrise till noon, rapt in a revery." Because his chronicles are so widely acclaimed, we think, *What a wonderful sentiment he expresses here.* But were our neighbor to seek this same reverie, we would criticize it as slothful. In contrast to Thoreau's love of a "broad margin," our modern view of time is to compress it and milk it for every nanosecond of productivity we can get.

To understand how a society experiences time, examine its operative vocabulary. We talk of no time, lack of time, not enough time, or being out of time. Trying to get more time, we borrow time only to incur a time debt and end up with even less time. Management in the workplace is so time-conscious that they practice time-management skills and time-compression techniques. They use a computerized timepiece to assure work efforts are time-intensive. This sense of time urgency creates time pressure and time stress.

If God would allow us to delete any of these time phrases we thought destructive, which would you choose? If you had the opportunity of setting the time agenda for society, which concepts of time would you endorse and which would you renounce? Many executives and type As would vote to keep time linked with speed and productivity. A typical manager's view of margin: If you can catch it, kill it.

The rest of us, however, would strike these time phrases from our collective vocabulary as mortifying to the human spirit. Of course work time is important. But so is discretionary time, that is, margin. Some discretionary time would be used as leisure time, free time, or time off. Some would be personal time, solitude time, fallow time, and time to think. We hope a good portion of it would be time together: sharing time, family time, couple time, prayer time.

Ideally, you see, our time should all be God's time, directed by Him and used for His purposes. It is not right that progress has tyrannized us so.

TIME AND TWITCHING

I have a fantasy: If a terrorist organization were to simultaneously trigger all the world's alarm clocks, stove timers, beepers, factory whistles, car horns, doorbells, digital-watch alarms, cellular phones, telephones, intensive-care alarms, smoke alarms, fire alarms, burglar alarms, civil-defense alarms, and sirens—namely, every manmade, adrenaline-shocking device that signals "Hurry!"—do you think it would be enough to bring Christ back prematurely out of sheer pity?

Have you ever had a beeper go off in your ear when you were sleeping? It is one of the most horrifying experiences ever dreamed up by technology to ambush innocent, already-exhausted wretches. Although it has happened to me thousands of times, to date I have not even begun to approach a psychic accommodation to the experience. It is fitting that a society with urgency as its emblem should have tranquilizers as its addiction. Where are the noises that tell us to slow down? Which way to Lake Wobegon, that "quiet town, where much of the day you could stand in the middle of Main Street and not be in anyone's way"?

Columnist Bob Greene called it the "twitching of America." Futurist David M. Zach called it "hyperliving—skimming along the surface of life." The late Norman Cousins called it "a sprinting, squirting, shoving age." From "fast food" to the "weekend squeeze" to the "Christmas rush," time has us in its grip.

CONFOUNDED SUNDIAL!

Long before our nanosecond culture, frustration with time urgency was apparent. Already in 200 BC, the Roman playwright Plautus was cursing the sundial.

> The gods confound the man who first found out
> How to distinguish hours! Confound him, too,
> Who in this place set up a sun-dial,
> To cut and hack my days so wretchedly
> Into small portions.[1]

Of course, time frenzy had barely begun, and were Plautus alive today he might run his chariot off a cliff. What was it like to have no notion of a second or a minute or even an hour? To never be late . . . or early. To never hear an alarm.

The first mechanical clocks were alarms of sorts, introduced in the Western world during the 1200s. Only a bell indicated time. In the 1300s, the dial and hour hand were added. "Here was man's declaration of independence from the sun, new proof of his mastery over himself and his surroundings," explains historian Daniel Boorstin. "Only later would it be revealed that he had accomplished this mastery by putting himself under the dominion of a machine with imperious demands all its own."[2]

By the 1600s, the minute and second hands were common. The invasion of the wristwatch began in 1865, about the same time Matthew Arnold penned his famous "The Scholar Gypsy."

> O born in days when wits were fresh and clear,
> And life ran gaily as the sparkling Thames;
> Before this strange disease of modern life,
> With its sick hurry, its divided aims,
> Its heads o'ertax'd, its palsied hearts, was rife —
> Fly hence, our contact fear!

In 1879, Thomas Edison produced the first electric light. If the clock broke up the day, the lightbulb broke up the night. Humanity was flushed with its presumed victory over yet another of nature's limitations. Yet all victories have their associated costs. The clock and the light—they gifted us with time, then they stole it away.

THE PREDICTION THAT TURNED OUT ALL WRONG

For much of the twentieth century, futurists and other labor experts were predicting ever shorter workweeks. In the mid-1920s, for example, Julian Huxley said that the two-day workweek was "inevitable" because of the simple fact that "the human being can consume only so much and no more." John Maynard Keynes observed in the early 1930s "when we reach the point when the world produces all the goods that it needs in two days, as it inevitably will . . . we must turn our attention to the great problem of what to do with our leisure."[3]

Forty years ago, futurists peering into their crystal balls were still predicting that one of the biggest problems for coming generations would be what to do with their abundant spare time. I remember hearing this prediction often. In 1967, for example, testimony before a Senate subcommittee claimed that by 1985 people could be working just twenty-two hours a week or twenty-seven weeks a year.[4]

Exactly when they stopped talking this way I am not sure, but they did stop. No one sits around today trying to figure out how to spend their free time. On the contrary, the topic of conversation is usually how to get some. Virtually everyone I know is time desperate.

Instead of falling as expected, the average American workweek has risen steadily the past several decades. Workers in the United States now lead the industrialized world in annual work hours. Overtime, moonlighting, second jobs, weekend work, and the dual-wage-earner family have all risen. One recent summer, our family took a sabbatical in Norway—where, at the time, the average Norwegian worker put in an astounding fourteen weeks per year *less* than the average U.S. worker (based on the forty-hour workweek). Norway, with a good work ethic and a very high standard of living, fourteen weeks less per year.

Table: *Annual Hours in the United States, 1967-2000* [5]

YEAR	ANNUAL HOURS
1967	1716
1973	1679
1979	1703
1989	1783
1995	1827
2000	1878

Note: The Key Indicators of the Labor Market (KILM) report of the International Labor Organization lists the U.S. worker hours in 2000 even higher at 1,978 hours annually.[6]

A 2002 report by the National Institute for Occupational Safety and Health indicates "that the average work year for prime-age working couples has increased by nearly 700 hours in the last two decades and that high levels of emotional exhaustion at the end of the workday are the norm for 25% to 30% of the workforce."[7]

Progress was billed as leisure-permitting and time-gifting. Somehow, the opposite has been true.

THE SPONTANEOUS FLOW OF PROGRESS

How can one explain this gap between the prediction and the reality? Instead of the workweek shrinking, it is expanding; instead of free time increasing, it is decreasing. And in spite of "time-saving" devices, we have less time.

To help us understand the answer, let's examine another axiom of progress:

Axiom #6: The spontaneous flow of progress is to consume more of our time, not less.

In other words, if we sit back and do nothing about it, next year at this time we'll have less time margin than we have right now. For every hour progress saves by organizing and technologizing our time, it consumes two more hours through the consequences, direct or indirect, of this activity. Because this fact is counterintuitive and subtle, we do not recognize it happening.

Even when progress does give us "leisure," the leisure is not leisurely. Instead, it is jammed with multi-tasking actions and expectations: watching TV while surfing the web while checking e-mail while eating a hamburger while listening to the phone ring while conversing with the family.

Observes Peggy Noonan, "So many of us feel we have no time to cook and serve a lovely three-course dinner, to write the long, thoughtful letter, to ever so patiently tutor the child. But other generations, not so long ago, did. And we have more timesaving devices than they did."[8]

"Paradoxical as it may seem, modern industrial society, in spite of an incredible proliferation of labor-saving devices, has not given people more time to devote to their all-important spiritual tasks; it has made it exceedingly difficult for anyone, except the most determined, to find any time whatever for these tasks," warned E. F. Schumacher, even decades ago. "In fact, I think I should not go far wrong if I asserted that the amount of genuine leisure available in a society is generally in inverse proportion to the amount of labor-saving machinery it employs."[9]

INTERRUPTIONS AND JUNK MAIL

Nearly all of us are caught scratching our heads about this mystery of having so little time in an era of so many conveniences and such vaunted efficiency. How can this be?

What did we do with all our time before we had traffic lights, stalled interstates, telephones and busy signals, televisions, interruptions, junk mail, committee meetings, and cluttered desks? What did we do with our time before we spent it shopping for things we don't need? What did we do with our time before we had to learn how to operate, on average, twenty thousand different pieces of equipment?

Is it possible the time was used for things more inherently valuable than commuter traffic, busy telephones, and junk mail? Is it possible the time was spent on things physically challenging instead of mentally frustrating? Is it possible the time was used for conversing, for serving, for resting, for praying?

True, we get to places faster—but we have more places to go. We have devices to help us clean—but we have more things stuffed into more square footage to clean. Hasn't the lightbulb given us more time because now we can plan activities during the evening that were previously limited to daylight hours? Yes. The lightbulb has given us more capacity to be busy, to produce, and to fill up schedules in the evening—when before all we could do was sit around the table and read or sit by the fire and read or sit with family and friends and visit until it was time to go to bed.

Let's revisit the Third World. Here we find no televisions, no shopping malls, no traffic lights, no telephones, no cluttered desks, no junk mail. So what do people do with their time? It exists for them as margin. Some of their time is used for work—the physical work of growing food, which is good for the body and spirit. Some of their time is used for visiting the marketplace, which is good for community. A good portion of their time is for leisure. Time to watch the kids play or the donkeys bray. Or to talk to the neighbor. Or to sleep.

WORK AND TIME STRESS

When we think of time pressure, perhaps no thought comes as quickly to mind as the workplace. When appropriately undertaken, work is biblically required and an absolute necessity for healthy living. Many, however, are so driven by their work that they can never take a day off or enjoy a quiet walk in the woods. Whether we call them "type A," "driven," "workaholic," or "extra effort people," they have a problem with work addiction. They do not notice the lack of balance in their lives, for they are too preoccupied with leading our national charge toward production, expansion, and success.

Such a drive toward accomplishment lands work-addicted people top positions in nearly every endeavor. From this vantage point they often systematically remove from their employees the same freedoms they themselves have forsaken. It is common to see a worker wishing for some measure of breathing space, yet gasping for freedom because of the demands of an excessively controlling boss. These employers are so affixed on success that their lives—and the lives of those they control—contain little besides work.

Meanwhile, for the exhausted, frustrated employee, there are three assignments due at the same time—yesterday. Deadlines flood over them like the Mississippi at springtime. They are on the road; then they are transferred. Debt and taxes mount, so they work harder. Family and friends become strangers passing in the night. First, they miss Johnny's home run and Betsy's first step. Then, they miss John's wedding and Elizabeth's graduation.

Because financial margin is often nonexistent, people seek supplemental employment. Many work two jobs or extra shifts. Work has invaded evenings, nights, weekends, holidays, and worship days. Stores and restaurants that once respected margin respect it no longer, often open twenty-four hours a day, 365 days a year.

Recently, however, as a result of this escalating work intensity, millions are choosing early retirement, and many millions more desperately wish that they could. Additionally, Americans are preferentially choosing leisure time with their families over work. In 1975, for example, 48 percent rated work as the important thing versus 36 percent for leisure. By 2000 the numbers had reversed—43 percent chose leisure and 34 percent work.[10] Upon first reflection, many might attribute this trend to laziness and lament it as reflective of all that is wrong with our country. But I see it as a corrective reaction to time starvation.

NANOSECOND EFFICIENCY

Improving productivity in the workplace is the equivalent of bodybuilding in the gym, and efficiency is the steroid. Bosses know that time pressure works, that it increases both productivity and efficiency. But who is to say when it has been pushed too far? Many video-display-terminal workers are now monitored electronically. Every keypunch is recorded, and if their quota is not met, their record is tainted and their job threatened.

Speed. Supercomputers operate at trillionths of a second. Do you know what that means? Neither do I, and I have a degree in physics. A trillionth of a second has no human reference.

Speed. Using electronic linkages, computers can make transactions so fast that the same dollars can finance seven different deals on the same day.

Speed. At international currency exchanges, traders watch their video-display screens as the constantly changing world-currency prices flash before them. If they move fast enough at the right moment, they can make hundreds of thousands of dollars in a couple of minutes.

Speed. In the past, it took weeks to send a letter by pony express. Then, it took days by mail. Then, hours by overnight jet. Now, it takes only seconds.

Speed and efficiency are the keys to productivity, and productivity is the key to success. But, of course, we must have quality. So we want more and more speed, more and more efficiency, more and more productivity, with better and better quality. In the end we have platinum products and dead workers.

"There is more to life," recognized Ghandi, "than increasing its speed."

TIME STRESS AND OUR FRIENDS

The marginless lifestyle and its resultant chronic time pressure are particularly devastating to our relationships: to self, to family, to others, to God.

Everyone needs personal time. Those who say they don't need time for self are probably the ones who need it the most. We all need time to let the dust settle, to evaluate how life is going, to plan for the future. "Those who are caught up in the busy life have neither the time nor quiet to come to understand themselves and their goals," explains Robert Banks. "Since the opportunity for inward attention hardly ever comes, many people have not heard from themselves for a long, long time. Those who are always 'on the run' never meet anyone any more, not even themselves."[11]

Everyone needs family time. Families have been particularly hard hit by the time famine. Nearly every study on family stress reveals time pressures to be at or near the top. Spouse-to-spouse time and parent-to-child quality time are often measured in mere minutes. "Making an appointment is one way to relate to your child," says anthropologist Peter Hammond, "but it's pretty desiccated. You've got to hang around with your kids."[12]

There are many tempting competitors for a parent's attention today, leaving us in a quandary about how much time and emotional energy we should give to child-rearing. "The inevitable loser from this life in the fast lane," explains psychologist Dr. James Dobson, "is the little guy who is leaning against the wall with his hands in the pockets of his blue jeans. Crowded lives produce fatigue—and fatigue produces irritability—and irritability produces indifference—and indifference can be interpreted by the child as a lack of genuine affection and personal esteem."[13] One professional couple whose junior high daughter needed psychiatric counseling, for example, had her driven weekly by taxi to see the doctor. For all involved, such busyness will end in tears.

Everyone needs sharing time. We each must have time to give away in the nourishing of our relationships. Calendars today are so crowded, however, that there is no space to pencil in a friend. As a result, long-term friendships are vanishing and neighborhood identities are fading. In the *Wall Street Journal* article "Whatever Happened to Friendship?" a New York executive says he just doesn't have time for friends anymore. With a wife, a young daughter and a busy job, "I'm already at 120%. There really is no room for anyone else."[14] Rather than the exception, this is the new normal, played out in every neighborhood of the nation.

Everyone needs God time. Because He is not pushy about His agenda, God is too easy to forget. He just waits . . . and waits. What does He think of "efficient" prayers? What happened to the "Be still and know that I am God" times? Societies that have the accelerator to the floor are doomed to become God-less. Speed does not yield devotion.

TIME AND THE INVENTOR OF TIME

Do you think Jesus would have carried a pocket calendar? Would He have consulted it before making commitments? Would He have bypassed the leper because His calendar said He was late for the Nazareth spring banquet?

Do you think Jesus would have worn a wristwatch? What would have been His reaction if the temple service extended past noon and alarms went off in the crowd? Would He have driven out the clock watchers along with the money changers? What would He have thought of the parishioner I knew who weekly timed the pastor's sermons with a stopwatch and reported the statistics on the way out of church?

Do you think Jesus would have carried a beeper? Would Martha and Mary have paged Him to come and raise Lazarus from the dead? Can you imagine Him being paged out of the Last Supper?

The clock and the Christ are not close friends. Imagine what God thinks of us now that we are so locked into schedules that we have locked ourselves out of the Sermon on the Mount—it is hardly possible to walk the second mile today without offending one's pocket calendar. We jump at the alarm of a Seiko but sleep through the call of the Almighty.

RESTORING TIME MARGIN

Progress tricked us into trusting it—then it exhausted us. But we are not helpless. The clock can be resisted. Time margin can be taken back. Let's see what steps we can take to restore sanity to our schedules.

Rx: 1 Expect the Unexpected

A proverb in Ecuador states: "Everything takes longer than it does." This is not a perfect world, and the unexpected happens. To plan for the unexpected is not an invitation to sloppiness or mediocrity but instead a concession to reality. If you want some breathing room, increase your margin of error.

Rx: 2 Learn to Say No

Because progress gives us more and more of everything faster and faster, the obvious result is steadily increasing options, opportunities, and obligations. Meanwhile, we are stuck with the 24-hour day. The inevitable collision between this escalating context and a fixed time frame catapults the word No to the front of the class.

Saying No is not just a good idea—it has now become a mathematical necessity. Without this two-letter word, I doubt that regaining margin is possible. If there are fifteen good things to do today and you can do only ten of them, you will need to say No five times. This is not rocket science but instead kindergarten logic. Yet saying No, for most of us, is enormously difficult.

When Steven Jobs took over Apple Computer for the second time in 1998, he preached that the company needed a prioritizing plan to rediscover its main emphasis. "Focus does not mean saying yes," explained Jobs, "it means saying no."[15] His words speak to many of our lives as well.

"No," says author Anne Lamott, "is a complete sentence." Speaking to a seminary graduation, she continued: "Believe me, we do not need hassled, bitter ministers. We don't want you to talk the talk about this being the day the Lord hath made and that we should rejoice and savor its beauty and poignancy when secretly you're tearing around like a white rabbit; we need you to walk the walk. And we need you to walk a little more slowly."[16]

One speaker told me she kept a "to-do" list and a "to-don't" list.

Saying No is not an excuse for selfishness, rudeness, or insensitivity. Instead, it is an invitation to listen carefully to the Spirit's voice, adhering closely to a system of wise priorities that inform our Yes and our No.

Rx: 3   Turn Off the Television

As long as you are saying No, say it to your television set. For the average adult, this would gain twenty to thirty hours a week. No other single effort will secure as much time margin as this simple, nearly impossible action.

Americans watch close to a billion hours of television *every day*. What did we do with this time before television was invented? Is it possible we lingered at the dinner table, helped the kids with homework, visited with the neighbors, dug in the garden, read great books, took long walks, and slept full nights?

One couple told me they put away the set every June 1 and get it out again on September 1. A nationwide movement suggests we turn it off for one week every year. Even Billy Graham, asked if starting over he'd do anything differently, said, "I'd watch less TV."

"I routinely require my students to engage in some kind of 'media fast,' in which they abstain from an electronic medium for at least one week," says seminary professor Douglas Groothuis. "The results have been nothing less than profound for the vast majority of the students. Having withdrawn from the world of TV, radio, computers, they find more silence, time for reflection and prayer, and more opportunities to engage family and friends thoughtfully."[17]

Rx: 4   Prune the Activity Branches

The fruit trees in our front yard grow new branches every spring. Counter-intuitively, if we want a healthy tree with better fruit, we need to prune away branches. In the same way, activities and commitments often have a way of adding themselves to our lives. Even though it is much harder to stop something than to start it, periodically, get out the clippers and prune away.

"I view my life as a tree," explains Jean Fleming. The trunk is the anchor of her life, her relationship to Christ. The limbs represent those major focus areas that God has given her—family, job, ministry, and personal development. And the branches represent the ever-proliferating multitude of activities. "Even without special care, activity branches multiply. Soon the profusion of branches becomes more prominent than the trunk and limbs. When this happens, I feel trapped, frustrated, and empty. Why? Because my life is shaped and drained by activities that have lost their pertinence to Christ."[18]

Rx: 5   *Practice Simplicity and Contentment*

We all consume significant quantities of time in the buying and then maintaining of things. A life of voluntary simplicity and contentment, on the other hand, is opposed to the unnecessary proliferation of material possessions. It is free of the clutter much of society must sort through on a daily basis. With fewer possessions, we do not have as many things to take care of. With a simpler wardrobe, our choice of what to wear each morning becomes less time-consuming. With a smaller estate, there will be less debt bondage in our work schedule.

Everything we own owns us. We must maintain it, paint it, play with it, build space in our house to put it, and then work to pay it off. Perhaps if we had fewer things we might have more time . . .

Recognize unnecessary possessions for what they are: stealers of divine time. At the beginning of every day we are given assignments that have eternal significance—to serve, to love, to obey, to pray. Instead, we squander much of this time on things that soon will leave us forever.

Rx: 6   *Separate Time from Technology*

The best thing to remember about time-saving technologies is that they don't. Instead, they consume, compress, and devour time. All the countries with the most time-saving technologies are the most stressed-out countries—an assertion that's easy to prove.

One Christian executive reports that he receives 1800 e-mails each day, while a Pentagon leader told me he had to do sixteen hours of e-mail *every* Saturday from home. While standing at the hospital bed of a dying man, a pastor interrupted his prayer to answer his cell phone. A youth pastor reported that he loved his job and tolerated long hours well—until he got home and routinely saw the answering machine blinking 9 messages. This escalating use of accessing technologies MUST be controlled, for the sake of our spirit and our sanity.

Remembering that technology is responsible for much of our time famine, it is good to go on strike occasionally. Try disconnecting from clocks, watches, alarms, beepers, telephones, and e-mail for a day, a weekend, or a week. Find the off switch. Don't answer the telephone. Stop giving people the number to your cell phone and instead use it to make calls rather than receive calls.

During a medical trip to the developing world my wristwatch of twenty years gave out. Upon return to the United States, I decided not replace it. Without a watch it is true that I was handicapped in a certain way. But it also gave an interesting sense of freedom. After a year, I finally purchased an inexpensive watch because my patients didn't quite know what to think of a doctor who had to borrow their watch to measure their pulse.

A man from Mali, West Africa told me "You Americans have all the watches, but we have all the time."

Rx: 7   Short-Term Flurry Versus Long-Term Vision

Americans are notoriously shortsighted. We live in a state of myopic mania that blurs the future. The horizon is never visible in the middle of a dust storm. But we must have a vision that extends beyond tomorrow. Living only from week-to-week is like a dot-to-dot life.

It is good to have five-year plans, even ten-year plans. For many these plans will be vague, for others specific. Our goals should be flexible to the redirecting God so often asks of us. But each of us needs a direction and a vision that can inform his or her focus.

Rx: 8   Thank God

If you have two meetings scheduled on the same evening, you obviously can attend only one. Don't overlook the possibility that this might be God's way of being kind to you.

Rx: 9   Sabotage Your Fuse Box

Have you ever noticed how a major storm freezes the clock? Time stands still as the whole world skids to a halt. The lights go out, and we rush for candles and flashlights. Then we sit and watch the sky or visit with each other or play board games. And sometimes we are tempted to pray that electricity isn't restored until a week from Tuesday.

Our family enjoys Wisconsin winters where a two-foot snowfall is a thrill, not a torment. When the world is snowed in, cars can't move, businesses can't open, and schools can't convene. A spirit of holiday reigns. Part of the reason for this is the unexpected gift of time margin.

"I'm not sure I understand it," commented Pastor Gordon MacDonald, "but I have this feeling that an increasing amount of conversational time between friends is spent on the subject of weariness, overcommitment, the perceived need to drop out. . . . Why on the one Sunday in five years when a New England snowstorm forced us to close down our church was it universally recognized by the congregation as the most wonderful Lord's day they had ever had?"[19]

Rx: 10 Get Less Done But Do the Right Things

Busyness is not a synonym for kingdom work—it is only busyness. All activities need to be assessed as to their spiritual authenticity. Again, if we have one hundred things to do and can do only ten, how do we select from among them? We must have God-authored criteria with which to judge our activities, and we must be willing to use them. "The goal of much that is written about life management is to enable us to do more in less time," writes Jean Fleming. "But is this necessarily a desirable goal? Perhaps we need to get *less done*, but the right things."[20]

"For many people," says pastor and author Rick Warren, "the barrier to spiritual growth is not lack of commitment, but overcommitment to the wrong things."[21] Especially be on guard against the urgency we see in so much of life's flow. If this urgency regularly erodes either your time for relationships or your time for rest, reevaluation is appropriate.

Rx: 11 Enjoy Anticipation, Relish the Memories

Calendar congestion and time urgency have robbed us of the pleasure of anticipation. Without warning, the activity is upon us. We rush to meet it; then we rush to the next. In the same way, we lack the joy of reminiscing.

On we fly to the next activity.

For this reason, our family plans fishing trips at least six months in advance. One trip to Alaska began with anticipation eighteen months in advance. You can't imagine how much fun we had just thinking and planning.

When the activity is over, remember. Tell stories. Tell them again. And again. Frame a picture. Mount a fish. Make a special effort to remember the funny happenings. With the gift of remembrance, we don't always have to do a lot. We can do a little and remember it a lot.

Rx: 12 Don't Rush Wisdom

Seldom is true wisdom a product of speedy deliberation. As a matter of fact, wisdom is almost always slow. Wait for clearness. The more important the decision, the longer the time you should take to make it.

If life's pace pushes you, push back. Take as much time and prayer as you need for clearness to develop. And wait for your decision to be affirmed by peace.

Rx: 13 For Type A's Only: Stand in Line

Cardiologist Dr. Meyer Friedman, one of the first to describe the type A personality, offered this practical advice to his patients: "Practice smiling. Purposely speak more slowly, stop in the middle of some sentences, hesitate for three seconds, then continue. Purposely say, 'I'm wrong' at least twice today, even if you're not sure you're wrong. Listen to at least two persons today without interrupting even once. . . . Seek out the longest line at the bank. Verbalize your affection to your spouse and children."

To the physician subset of type A's (a large subset), he suggests, "Trash the extraneous. Cut out some of the committees, perhaps all. Give yourself a lunch break—out of the office. Browse in a bookstore, sit in a deserted church, go to a museum. During office hours, have your secretary schedule imaginary patients, whose names you don't know. Naturally, these patients will be no-shows. You will be able to use that time to catch up . . . or best of all, renew your spirit."[22]

Rx: 14 *Create Buffer Zones*

If you have a busy schedule with nonstop appointments, consider creating small buffer zones between some of the obligations, a kind of coffee break for the spirit. Even ten or fifteen minutes can allow you to catch up, take a deep breath, close your eyes, pray, call your spouse, reorient your priorities, and defuse your tension.

Rx: 15 *Plan for Free Time*

If God were our appointment secretary, would He schedule us for every minute of every day? Well-meaning Christians might differ in their answers, but by now it must be obvious that I think the answer would be no. Many arguments could be made in defense of my answer, but perhaps the strongest is the lifestyle that Christ Himself chose. Time urgency was not only absent, it was *conspicuously* absent. And I doubt its absence had to do with cultural context.

Christ's teaching, His healing, His serving, and His loving were usually spontaneous. The person standing in front of Him was the opportunity He accepted. If He chose spontaneous living, isn't that a signal to us? Overloaded schedules are not the way to walk *In His Steps*.

Rx: 16 *Be Available*

Margin exists for the needs of the kingdom, for the service of one another, for the building of community. It exists, just as we exist, for the purpose of being available to God.

"But it is possible that the most important thing God has for me on any given day is not even on my agenda," observes Pastor Bruce Larson. "Am I interruptible? Do I have time for the nonprogrammed things in my life? My response to those interruptions is the real test of my love."[23]

Being useful to God and other people is a large part of what life is meant to be. And yet "usefulness is nine-tenths availability." When others need help, they don't need it two days from now. "We must be ready to allow ourselves to be interrupted by God," explained Dietrich Bonhoeffer. "God will be constantly crossing our paths and canceling our plans by sending us people with claims and petitions. . . . It is part of the discipline of humility that we must not spare our hand where it can perform a service and that we do not assume that our schedule is our own to manage, but allow it to be arranged by God."[24]

DO YOURSELF A FAVOR

When flying from New York to San Francisco, we don't allow only three minutes to change planes in Chicago. A much greater margin of error is needed. But if we make such allowances in our travels, why don't we do it in our living? Life is a journey, but it is not a race. Do yourself a favor and slow down.

It is not easy to reassert our right to time margin, but it helps when we are convinced that legitimacy exists for such a right. This legitimacy comes from the same God who exalts faithfulness over productivity and availability over schedulability. It comes from the same God who invented time in the first place and reserves the right to set the rules for its use.

God never intended for time to oppress us, dictating our every move. That was progress's idea. Instead, time was simply His way of making sure "everything didn't happen all at once." We are free to use it, and if we are wise, we will use it with eternity in view.

Regaining margin in our use of time is one way of restoring freedom to overloaded lives. With time margin we can better enjoy what we are doing, we have a more wholesome anticipation of our next activity, we are more contemplative, we are more in touch with God and with each other, we have more time for service, and we actually delight in looking for the divine interruptions He sends us.

MARGIN IN FINANCES

MOIRA WAS A forty-year-old psychology professor from Texas. I first saw her during the second year of my residency training where we met over her gall bladder symptoms. Several visits later, her symptoms persisting, we decided on surgery. After a thorough history and physical, I predicted a successful operation followed by an inevitable demise. I was right. Her demise, however, was not physical but fiscal.

Moira and her husband had no children. In substitute, they had seven cars, two boats (one that never touched water), a hot-air balloon, and a home with four thousand square feet of living space chock-full of brand-new clutter.

After bankruptcy proceedings, I happened to meet Moira downtown. "We are leaving for Texas next week," she smiled. "I was able to get a good job down there. The Lord has been good to us." I had never heard her talk about the Lord before and wondered about her theology. I also wondered if she had paid the clinic bill.

Both Moira and her husband worked. I never knew how much money they made. But however much it was, they spent more.

THE BEST OF TIMES AND THE WORST OF TIMES

Every year, Americans spend more on eating out than the individual gross national product of 207 countries in the world. Wealth. Is it the blessing of a generous God, or the fast track to spiritual ruin? Are we to feel guilt for the trash we put in our plastic bags or gratitude for the pizza and prime rib?

Our unprecedented affluence has brought benefits that even the most cynical ought to acknowledge. We have been able to afford education, housing, extended communications, and transportation to just about anywhere. We have health-care advancements that free us from grievous disease. Our food is plenteous. Recreational options seem limited only by the imagination. The elderly are, by and large, better-off financially than they have ever been. We even have enough to be generous benefactors, privately and governmentally, to the impoverished at home and abroad. It is clearly the best of times.

Unfortunately, however, these benefits do not constitute the whole story; luminous advancements often cast dark shadows. In the case of our economic prosperity, the shadows of debt, vulnerability, and uncertainty extend far into the future. For every positive economic indicator, there is a corresponding dismal one. We are in troubled water on nearly every financial front, and no one can confidently suggest a way out. "Serious economic experts make predictions that come up inside out," observes Norman Mailer, "and no one can quite explain why they are wrong."[1]

The major parameters of economic well-being fluctuate up and down, up and down, while millions of people nervously await each new development. How did we ever come to this state of dependence on the economy? The question ought not to be "What are the economic statistics doing?" but instead "What are the economic statistics doing to us?" Is the economy freeing us physically and spiritually and granting us a financial margin with which to serve the purposes of God? Or are we being reduced to feverish bundles of nervousness, discontent, and greed?

BEYOND OUR MEANS

Despite our bounty, our list of economic woes is a long one. The ever-expanding invoice of problems requires an ever-expanding ocean of money, yet our government—along with a huge percentage of its citizens—is broke.

- Personal/household, national, and international debt levels are lofting through the stratosphere.
- Bankruptcies are at record levels, well exceeding one million each year.
- Unemployment figures are both volatile and unpredictable, job stability is tenuous, and international outsourcing of labor is increasingly common.
- Real estate costs have inflated alarmingly.
- College tuition costs have consistently outpaced inflation to the point where parents can no longer afford the fees. Student borrowing has skyrocketed.
- Scandal and greed rock the corporate world.
- Many cities and states are straining under debt pressure.
- Health-care spending continues to spiral out of control. Federal agencies estimate that total health-care spending will rise to a staggering $3.1 trillion by 2012.

We are not running out of urgent projects that need expensive attention, but we are quickly running out of funding resources. When baby boomers begin retiring around 2010, the fiscal math may well slip into a black hole. Funding health care and pension funds are already a major corporate and federal problem. Yet there is very little realistic policy in place now to address the looming fiscal realities of our near future. It is too easy politically to worsen tomorrow's problems in order to win today's votes.

DEBT WRONG

Significant controversy exists among economic experts concerning the advisability of debt. Some argue that debt is the only effective restraint on congressional spending. Additionally, many economists believe that as long as indebtedness does not grow faster than the gross national product, it can prove beneficial to the performance of the economy. This is especially true if the debt, rather than wasted on consumption, is invested in our future, such as research and development, infrastructure improvement, and education.

Others remain unconvinced. Debt, they say, unavoidably imprisons the future, and the "buy now, pay later" mentality too often corrupts into "binge now, pain later." The debt trap set for us has a sudden spring, one that cuts off financial margin at the neck.

Debt-sponsored economic theory has only been around for about seventy years. Deeply troubled by the unemployment of the Great Depression, Britisher John Maynard Keynes began urging governments to abandon Adam Smith's laissez faire approach and to become more active in regulating the economy, especially to avoid or reverse downturns. This led to the notion that it is acceptable and even fiscally wise for borrowing, credit, and interest to fuel an economy. President Franklin D. Roosevelt had no objection, for after all, we were only borrowing it from ourselves.

As a result, the national debt began its growth in the 1930s, followed by corporate debt after 1945. Shortly thereafter, personal debt began to swell. And in the mid-1980s, our international trade deficit turned negative for the first time since 1917. So much capital is now being siphoned off for interest payments that the entire economic system is increasingly threatened with paralysis.

For my part, I don't like debt. Debt is a noose, and I don't like having my neck in a noose. I don't like my future being imprisoned. I don't like the idea that my children and my children's children will hold me to blame for their suffering. But I am not in charge, and by now, debt—that sworn enemy of margin—is everywhere.

"Let no debt remain outstanding, except the continuing debt to love one another," the apostle Paul reminds us in Romans.[2] "God doesn't prohibit borrowing," explains Larry Burkett, "but He certainly does discourage it. In fact, every biblical reference to it is negative."[3] Why? Because, as Proverbs explains, "The borrower is servant to the lender."[4] After God paid so dearly to free us, He would prefer we not become slaves again except to righteousness.[5]

I am not an economist and can feel Luther Hodge's breath on my ear: "If ignorance paid dividends most Americans could make a fortune out of what they don't know about economics." But I would be less than honest if I didn't admit that the practice of chronic indebtedness at such levels seems unwise to me. Admittedly, this rather old-fashioned conviction might never lead to riches, but then, I don't remember Christ signaling me in that direction anyway.

PLASTIC AND THE PIT

Spending more than we make is one of those modern plastic privileges of dubious advantage. Much of this deficit spending on a personal and family level occurs because buying has become a national mania. According to studies, one-third of all shoppers experience an "irresistible compulsion" to buy. Many buy strictly out of impulse. They go to the mall with nothing in mind other than recreational shopping. Not only is it entertaining, but it makes them feel better—an antidepressant of sorts.

Credit cards are a ubiquitous presence in this debt temptation—easy to obtain, easy to use, and hard to pay off. On the front side, this kind of credit is seductive. Out the back door, however, it is treacherous. Credit cards give the perception of prosperity but the reality of impoverishment. The innocent-appearing plastic card draws its life from our financial margin, becoming more powerful as we sink deeper into debt. Soon we find ourselves looking up from a deep hole, surrounded by possessions we do not really own. "We can be poor because of the things we have," suggests William T. Snyder. "In debt and committed to the hilt, living from one paycheck to the next means a person has no room to wiggle!"[6]

Our love affair with plastic is one of the main reasons we have "no room to wiggle," that is, no margin. Yet we have lost interest in the discussions about caution and restraint. When it comes to fiscal matters, our skills at rationalization are so well developed we scarcely wince when God's Word counters us. We may soon learn that we followed the wrong piper, not to Paradise but to the pit.

Wealth

"Money," the Yuppie maxim goes, "is life's report card." Our society is so captivated with earning money, having money, and spending money that we can think of little else. And what better way to gain a financial margin than to earn more money! But just as riches are not righteousness, so money is not margin.

Nothing in Scripture and in the chosen lifestyle of Christ could be clearer: Wealth is not a primary objective of the spiritual life. When we encounter money along the path of life, we are encouraged to do one of three things with it: turn and walk in the other direction; pick it up and give it away; or use it for the necessities of daily living. Any other interaction risks adverse spiritual consequences.

"Do not store up for yourselves treasures on earth. . . . But store up for yourselves treasures in heaven," Jesus taught. "For where your treasure is, there your heart will be also."[7] He, in fact, spent a great deal of time expounding on the issue, discussing it even more than the topic of prayer. If the ultimatum "You cannot serve both God and Money" was relevant for ancient Israel, how much more for our modern world?

Paul adds his warning in the strongest terms: "People who want to get rich fall into temptation and a trap and into many foolish and harmful desires that plunge men into ruin and destruction. . . . Some people, eager for money, have wandered from the faith and pierced themselves with many griefs. But you, man of God, flee from all this, and pursue righteousness, godliness, faith, love, endurance and gentleness."[8]

Again and again the Word instructs us in explicit terms to distrust money. It is not that money is evil, but that the love of money leads to all kinds of evil. With sufficient wisdom and discipline, money can glorify God and be a blessing to many. But wisdom and discipline are not exactly our long suit.

The Investment Firm of John and John

I am not a wealthy man, and I will never be a wealthy man. This statement arises not from an inability to generate wealth. In fact, my various professional endeavors have well-recognized income-generating abilities. It is not that I am *unable* to be wealthy, but rather I am *unwilling* to be wealthy. Why would I wish to fall into a trap, be plunged into ruin and destruction, be pierced with many griefs, and risk wandering from the faith?

In my own heart, where these things must ultimately be decided, I feel deeply the words of the apostle John: "If anyone has material possessions and sees his brother in need but has no pity on him, how can the love of God be in him?"[9] That particular verse has dwelt with Linda in a closely bound friendship since her college days. Additionally, we are convicted by the example of John Wesley, who said, "If I leave behind me ten pounds for which I have no use I am a thief and a robber." It just seems to me that, according to the investment firm of John and John, we should keep our needs low, our generosity high, and our expectations heavenward.[10]

We only buy older cars and seldom buy new clothes. We eat simply, and Linda bakes almost daily. She cuts my hair. I don't own a suit and even though traveling and speaking around the nation and the world, I get by with one sport coat. We cut and burn wood to supplement our gas furnace, and we survive without central air conditioning. We often buy used books. Our fishing boat is 1950s vintage. Yet we have a rich and fulfilling life in every way.

FOR THE FUN OF IT

Any discussion of financial margin would be incomplete without mentioning the pure joy of it. There are three reasons for this joy.

First, by lowering expenses below income you live with far less stress and pressure. If the refrigerator breaks down, you don't. If your car needs new tires, you simply go out and get them. Without margin, life struggles and staggers and stumbles. But when margin is present, life flows. And flowing is more enjoyable than staggering.

Second, having financial margin allows beneficence toward others. This is one of the most rewarding of all human activities, and I am convinced it is a subset of love. Meeting the needs of others delivers us from the world of selfishness and into a world of grace and gratitude.

These two sources of joy are sufficient grounds to recommend margin. But there is yet a third, even greater, source of joy. It is a transcendent kind of pleasure that comes neither from within nor without but from above. It comes from the source of all that is right, and when you approach it you feel its warmth even from a distance. In giving, you are ushered into a world where cynicism and hatred have been banished. You are considering others before yourself. You are choosing heaven as the place you will put your treasure. You are doing what God asked you to do, and what He did Himself. In giving, you are pleasing Him.

"It is more blessed to give than to receive," Jesus taught us through Paul. These words are not talking about a future-tense, theoretical blessing waiting for us beyond the eternal horizon, reserved there as compensation for the excruciating pain of giving today. Instead, this is a kind of joy that begins with the thought of giving, with the declaration of freedom in your soul that indeed you belong to God. And the joy culminates in the act of giving, often a secret except for the spotlight of heaven.

The German existentialist Friedrich Nietzsche once claimed that Christians have no joy. But joy is mentioned over five hundred times in Scripture and clearly ought to be a part of the normal Christian life. If you wince because Nietzsche's dagger finds a joyless heart, restore your financial margin and then give it away.

RESTORING FINANCIAL MARGIN

Many see no way out. They have been treading water so long that they can't remember what it was like to have money left at the end of the month. They are controlled. Mammon, it seems, has won.

For all such weary debtors, take hope. A solution for our many economic burdens is possible; otherwise, God is not God. Let's see how we might go about restoring margin to our finances.

Rx: 1 *Travel in the Right Direction*

When making a journey of known destination, it is important to start out on the right road headed in the right direction. In this case, our destination is restored financial margin. But before beginning our trip, the Father has some travel instructions.

If consulted, God would probably vote in favor of each of the previous three margins: emotional energy, physical energy, and time. Regarding financial margin, however, He would furrow His brow, look us in the eye, and then respond, "It depends." The issue hinges on whether or not the desired financial margin honors Him. Although each of the four margins discussed can be misused for self-serving goals, destinations involving money are particularly famous for dishonoring God. He wants to be sure before casting His vote with us.

In dealing with money, settling the issue of lordship is a mandatory first step. Otherwise, we find ourselves headed off in the wrong direction and mired in a spiritual morass that I want no part of. So, to clarify, we are not talking about restoring financial margin for the purposes of pride, of wealth, or of meeting our security needs in a way that bypasses the Father. Instead, we are talking about the kind of financial margin that honors Him.

To reach this kind of financial margin, which direction do we travel? The choice of nearly the entire Western world is to travel down the economic road. Economists and politicians of the past fifty years have honestly believed that economic advancement was the solution to the problems of humankind—a view shared nearly universally today. The conveniences I enjoy make me a beneficiary of such thinking. Yet if we are honest with ourselves, we should admit that the economic road was never suggested to us by Christ.

"Most of what people really want in life—love, friendship, respect, family, standing, fun—is not priced and does not pass through the market," explains Gregg Easterbrook. "If something isn't priced you can't buy it, so possessing money may not help much."[11] In our modern mind-set, however, all roads lead to the market.

Economics will solve some of our suffering, but nothing more. Solving our suffering is not necessarily the goal of the Christian life; walking in righteousness is. If we suffer, then we suffer—it is only for a season. But the economic road is not the road. The proverbial "bottom line" is not, after all, the bottom line.

If we are to restore margin to our finances, we must put first things first. Only then will we be able to break the power money holds on us and use it instead of being used by it.

Rx: 2   Break Its Back

Money is powerful. It is so powerful, taught Jesus, that it competes head-to-head with God. "For Mammon's work is the exact opposite of God's work," explains French sociologist Jacques Ellul. "Given this opposition, we understand why Jesus demands a choice between Mammon and God. He is not speaking of just any other power, just any other god; he is speaking of the one who goes directly against God's action, the one who makes 'nongrace' reign in the world."[12]

Before we can accomplish anything righteous with money, we first need to understand this power, confront it, and with the help of God, demolish it. How is it possible to break the substantial power money holds over us? Very simple—give it away. "There is one act par excellence which profanes money by going directly against the law of money, an act for which money is not made," says Ellul. "This act is GIVING."[13]

When we give money away, we not only neutralize its power over us, but we also bring it under the domain of the Kingdom of Light. Nongrace is turned into grace. God is honored, and His lordship is confirmed.

Rx: 3   Counter Culture

Once we are headed in the right direction and have broken the power money holds over us, then we find yet another important battle in front of us: We must break the power of culture.

The way of the world is not a benign force, but instead a dictator that tells us how much education we should have; what kind of job we should seek; what kind of house, car, and clothes we should buy; who is "beautiful" and who isn't. It is rare to meet a person who isn't owned, bound, or trapped in destructive ways by a multitude of controlling cultural forces.

If we remain controlled by such a culture, we will have little chance of achieving God-honoring financial margin. That same culture will demand we buy its wares and live by its rules. Acquiescing to such demands inevitably leads to margin erosion.

Willingly and knowingly we wrestle control from culture and set our orientation in the opposite direction. It is wonderful if a community of believers can support one another in making such countercultural decisions. But don't wait for your friends or fellow churchgoers to lead the way or even to give you permission. This is a battle you must fight, and unfortunately, often you will need to fight it alone.

Rx: 4 "Live Within Your Harvest"

As the proverb suggests, make do with what you have. And, should you care to venture further into grace, not only make do with what you have but accept what you have. More than a strategy, this is a conviction, the kind where you drive a stake and declare it so.

Living within your harvest is possible — it just isn't popular. It conveys that we have boundaries and that we are willing to confine ourselves within the scope of these boundaries rather than pine for the putative greener grass on the other side of the fence.

Contentment and simplicity are invaluable friends in this effort, as we will see in the next two chapters. Content yourself with what God sends your way and live a simple life of righteousness. Then God, honored by your devotion, will in turn tend to both your margin and your harvest.

Rx: 5 Discipline Desires and Redefine Needs

There is great confusion as to how we distinguish needs from desires. The list of what we call "needs" today is certainly much longer than the list was in 1900, which in turn was much longer than the list at the time of Christ. If the list expands each year, is this an expansion God approves of? "The cultivation and expansion of needs is . . . the antithesis of freedom," teaches economist E. F. Schumacher. "Every increase of needs tends to increase one's dependence on outside forces over which one cannot have control."[14]

It is wise to clarify this distinction between needs and desires and to be honest about it before God. Our true needs are few and basic: We need God, love, relationships, meaningful work, food, clothing, and shelter. Most of the rest of what we call needs are instead desires, relative to the age and location in which we live.

Let me quickly state that I don't think God limits us to only our needs. He is a generous, gracious God who allows us many of our desires. So if I want carpeting in my house, I should not attempt to deceive God or myself by calling it a need. But I should also realize that God is generous and might well grant the desire.

The issue is knowing when God says "Thus far and no more." For me, when there is pride, ostentation, laziness, waste, or excessive comfort involved, then it is a desire I don't even try to bring before God.

We are greatly aided if we tune out advertisements, which are nothing more than "need creation." If we listen to them, our financial margin will disappear as we chase a satiation we'll never find.

Rx: 6   Decrease Spending

Coming now to perhaps the more practical aspects of this topic, there are three ways to increase our financial margin: decrease spending, increase income, or increase savings. Among these choices, the best is to simply reduce spending. It sounds easy, but as we all know, in practice it's hard to sustain. The context of our culture screams against restraint, and every message we receive—from the ads on television to the specials in the newspaper to our neighbor's new van—all urge us to cave in.

A friend, who at one time owned a catalog store, offered this interesting explanation of customer spending patterns: "When people run out of money, they stop shopping. But this only lasts about six weeks. Then, whether their financial situation has improved or not, they start buying again."

Doesn't that match what we know to be true about human nature? Understanding this simple fact of human psychology leaves us in a stronger position than we were before. We now recognize that even our best resolves usually last only a short time and require conscious renewal on a regular basis.

There are two facets of decreased spending: short-term and long-term. Even a short-term spending freeze—a day, a week, a month—is helpful in reestablishing financial margin. In contrast, the long-term approach requires a vastly different level of commitment and is better thought of as a lifestyle change. Short-term resolves are considerable in number but limited in effect; long-term resolves are limited in number but considerable in effect. For example, a moratorium on eating out for a month is sustainable and would improve the average family's financial margin by $100-200. But a decade-long moratorium on eating out would be very difficult for most families, even though it would improve their financial margin by $10,000-20,000.

Rx: 7   *Increase Income*

Increasing income by increasing work hours is a common approach used to solve financial problems. In some instances, this is appropriate. In other situations, however, it only compounds marginless living. As we saw in the last chapter, most of us already have a shortage of discretionary time and are not looking to increase work hours. Yet desperation and a perceived need to consume more cause people to do strange things.

We see service-sector workers who volunteer for overtime or weekends; farmers who are now milking three times a day in an effort to increase production; spouses who violate their personal convictions to enter the dual-wage-earner role; executives who accept a promotion they don't really want; medical residents who moonlight covering emergency rooms. In each instance, these workers would rather have more time margin than more work. But their financial margin has been so eroded that they seem to no longer have a choice.

Here we need to reconsider the issue of *needs* versus *desires*. Many people work extra and then four months later buy a new car. They have made their choices and do not have my sympathy. Others have indeed trimmed both needs and desires to bare bones. For them, increasing income seems the only option left.

The tendency of choosing more work hours in order to increase financial margin has a significantly negative effect on our time margin. On occasion, we observe that our quest for margin collides with itself, one need against the other.

Rx: 8   Increase Savings

Increasing savings is yet a third way of maintaining a financial margin. If, for example, you currently have no savings and pay expenses from a checking account that is monthly drained dry, what happens if there are emergency medical expenses? You would need to take out a loan and enter into debt. But if you sustained a savings, you would have margin against such emergencies.

Unscheduled and unpredictable breakdowns will happen, and we should consider having some margin for them to happen in. Appliances, automobiles, lawn mowers—all wear out, usually on their own timetable. Sickness, unemployment, and sudden travel expenses are other unanticipated events. With budgets already stretched to the limits, such emergencies often result in a fiscal crisis.

Most Christian financial counselors recommend a regular savings program: for children's college education, for exceptional medical expenses, for housing costs, for retirement. In addition, some advisors recommend setting aside a contingency fund equal to three to six months of your usual spending for unexpected emergencies. I personally do not follow this rule, preferring to live closer to the edge of faith.

In the final analysis, the issue is not savings but hoarding. Moderate savings is probably acceptable to God and a good component of financial margin. Hoarding, however, is never acceptable. He is trusting us with certain resources; He as owner and we as stewards. We should never pretend that we have rights to what is not ours.

God is honored by funnels and dishonored by sponges. Be a conduit of His blessing, not a dead end.

Rx: 9   Make a Budget

Making a budget has the distinction of enjoying the most universal recommendation of all financial counselors. The scope of this book does not yield itself to the specifics of how to make a budget, and there are many other books available to teach that. But if you have trouble in the area of financial margin, the first thing you should do is to set up a budget.

Rx: 10 Discard Credit Cards

The second action is to cut up your credit cards. The majority of American families would probably be better-off if credit cards disappeared from the face of the earth tomorrow. They can be extremely dangerous.

To be honest, I do not believe all credit cards need to be thrown away, and I personally have credit cards. I use them for traveling and because I seldom carry much cash. But I would recommend not having credit cards if you are prone to impulse buying, if you already have excessive amounts of consumer debt, or if you cannot pay off the balance each month.

For a fairly large percentage of people, nothing would regain their financial margin faster than the simple act of destroying all their credit cards and instead paying cash for purchases.

Rx: 11 Don't Mortgage the Future

Financial counselors advise against assuming a mortgage of more than 40 percent of net spendable income. (The net spendable income equals the gross income minus the taxes and tithe.) Included in this percentage are not only the mortgage payments but also the real estate taxes, insurance, utilities, and repairs.

Obviously, the smaller the percentage you spend on mortgage and associated costs, the larger your financial margin. Forty percent is a ceiling. Also, if you have other concurrent nonmortgage debts, this percentage may need to be decreased.

Far too many people, especially young couples, take on a mortgage that effectively deprives them of any financial margin for decades to come. When the hard reality sets in, they worry, they develop conflicts in their marriage, they begin overworking to try to make ends meet, and they deprive themselves of the joy of giving to the unexpected needs God sends their way.

Rx: 12 Resist Impulses

A large percentage of purchases are made on sheer impulse, which is why stores stack impulse items near the cash register. These are the things you didn't go to the store to buy but bought anyway. If you want financial margin, don't buy on impulse. Buy only those things you know you need and can use. If you have difficulty in this area, make a list of needed items before going to the store and don't deviate from it.

It goes without saying that big-ticket items, such as a car, boat, or house, should *never* be bought on impulse.

Rx: 13 *Share, Lend, Borrow*

Part of our love affair with shopping and consumerism is because we think we need to personally own everything we use. This is not true. We need to develop a new *depreciation* of things and a new *appreciation* of people. Things are to be used, and people are to be served. To not allow someone to use something we own places more importance on the thing than on the person. It is a common error in our society, and one that particularly dishonors God. He feels our neighbors are so valuable that He sent His Son to die for them. But we think so little of our neighbors that we won't let them use our lawn mower. These attitudes are literally an eternity apart.

When I brought my chain saw in for repairs, the attendant offered his philosophy on lending: "Never loan out your chain saw. Other people don't take care of it." Nonsense. I haven't seen my chain saw now for the last twelve months, and I'm not worried a bit. As a matter of fact, I can't think of anything I own that I would not be willing to lend to another person. Of course, I have somewhat of an advantage in that I do not have fancy or expensive things.

If we are willing to loan our things, then others will not need to purchase similar items. All are benefited.

Rx: 14 *Emphasize Usefulness over Fashion*

The out-of-control fashion games we play also rob us of freedom, destroy our peace, and deprive us of financial margin. Some fool halfway around the world proclaims we must wear purple shirts and blue tennis shoes this year. Like robots we respond in unison.

Someone has to give permission for people not to follow fashion. The opinion levied over and over again by culture says that if you wear plain clothes and drive a rusty car, you should feel embarrassed. But God never said such a thing at all. As individuals and as churches, we ought to be saying the same things that God says. Does your church give people permission to live simply and not feel embarrassed? If not, then begin doing something about it. I don't mean in an institutional way that would risk legalism. Instead, begin doing something in a personal way. Go to the cross, take the embarrassment yourself, and start allowing others to follow your example of simplicity in fashion.

Rx: 15 Fast

It is healthy to periodically separate from the things of the world and do without. In traditional thinking, such fasting pertains to food. But in the context of financial margin, it is good to fast from shopping for periods of time. Use up what you have in the refrigerator and freezer. Wear out whatever clothes you have in the closet. Get along on whatever you have in the house. Remember the sampler on Grandma's kitchen wall: "Use it up. Wear it out. Make it do. Do without."

The world does not stop nor the family fall apart when we unplug from the treadmill of consumerism for a period. About the only momentous thing that will happen is your finances will be resuscitated by a much-needed transfusion of margin.

Rx: 16 Kingdom First

Jesus was distinctly unambiguous when teaching about priorities: "But seek first the kingdom of God and His righteousness, and all these things shall be added to you."[15]

All margins—in emotional energy, in physical energy, in time, and especially in finances—ought to fall within this context. All margins ought first to honor God. All margins ought to be made available for the purposes of His kingdom.

Money belongs to God. Wealth belongs to God. The kingdom belongs to God. We belong to God. Margin belongs to God.

Only the choice belongs to us.

PART THREE

THE PROGNOSIS

HEALTH

HEALTH THROUGH CONTENTMENT

SOME PUBLIC HEALTH authorities estimate that only 10 percent of the indicators of health are influenced by physicians, hospitals, and medicines. What, then, influences the other 90 percent? This book is about the building of a new, integrated health paradigm, beginning with margin. Margin—its presence or absence—influences health. Restoring margin is a huge first step in the health direction. At least we can breathe again.

But margin cannot survive standing on its own. Too many forces come against it. Attempting to build a margined life without support is like attempting to build a tree house without a tree. The tree house might be just what you need for protection against the dangers of the jungle. But it must have a tree.

Contentment is willing to lend support to margin. So are simplicity, balance, and rest. Without this help, margin has little chance of surviving. These four builders of health, however, are not very popular today. They are meek and unpretentious, greatly overshadowed by the flamboyant power of progress.

INEXTINGUISHABLE DISCONTENT

Half a century ago, my grandfather might reasonably have predicted that advances in affluence, technology, education, and entertainment would bring a commensurate increase in contentment. Such has not been the case. Instead, observes historian Arthur M. Schlesinger, Jr., our society is marked by "inextinguishable discontent." Discontent has become a way of life. When we are told this is "the age of envy," the indictment does not sting. When E. F. Schumacher accuses our economic system of using "greed and envy as its motive power," our response is to yawn and dial our broker.

Contentment is a cause without a constituency, a virtue without a voice. No one talks about it, let alone recommends it. Books dedicated to it are rare. I cannot recall the last sermon I heard addressing it. Why isn't it emphasized within the church as it is in the Scriptures?

Discontent as a driving force for a society might make that society rich, but it will bankrupt it in the end. As the coffer fills, the soul empties. It's like planting a garden with weeds. Come July there will be plenty of green, but in September we'll have nothing to eat.

THE SECRET

Contentment is not only a good idea, it is our duty. If God recommends something, we ought to do it. If God requires something, we must do it. As J. I. Packer has emphasized, contentment is both commended ("Godliness with contentment is great gain") and commanded ("Be content with what you have").[1]

Such a forceful endorsement by the Almighty should make contentment a prominent concern for each of us. Instead, we make it a secret concealed by our indifference. When the apostle Paul wrote, "I have learned the secret of being content," his use of the word secret was intentional.[2] Those things we expect to bring contentment surprisingly do not. We cannot depend upon it to fall into place through the progressive evolving of civilization, for contentment arises from a different source.

Most of us do not know how to uncover this secret and have never seriously tried. Our quest is usually not for *contentment* but for *more*. This quest brings us into an immense maze, where before us lie dozens of avenues. Some are wide, luxurious, and tempting, and we see a rush of our friends entering them. They lead to beautiful houses, comfortable cars, exotic vacations, and affluence. Other avenues, equally popular, lead to prestigious colleges, distinguished jobs, important friends, and power. Still others direct us to beautiful spouses, beautiful children, deep tans, and popularity.

All the while, off to one side, courses a narrow uphill road, unadorned and unpopular. It is dusty from sparse use and lonely from lack of travelers. The sole treasure at its end is an elusive commodity called "godliness with contentment."

Godliness is an attitude whereby what we want is to please God.

Contentment, explains J. I. Packer, "is essentially a matter of accepting from God's hand what He sends because we know that He is good and therefore it is good."[3]

Contentment is the freedom that comes when prosperity or poverty do not matter; to accept what we have and "to want but little," as Thoreau advised. The more we choose contentment, the more God sets us free. The more He sets us free, the more we choose contentment.

FORTY LASHES MINUS ONE

The apostle Paul lived in such a state of freedom, but that did not spare him pain. He suffered much for his faith—even more than most other martyrs. "It seems to me," he writes, "that God has put us apostles on display at the end of the procession, like men condemned to die in the arena. We have been made a spectacle to the whole universe. . . . We are weak. . . . We are dishonored! To this very hour we go hungry and thirsty, we are in rags, we are brutally treated, we are homeless. . . . We have become the scum of the earth, the refuse of the world."[4]

Comparing himself to those who boast of their spirituality, Paul further points out that he had worked harder, been in prison more often, been flogged and exposed to death many times. He had received forty lashes minus one on five occasions, been beaten with rods, three times been shipwrecked, been in the open sea overnight, been hungry, thirsty, cold, and naked, and gone without sleep again and again.[5]

Despite his suffering, Paul teaches us about the secret we need. From prison he writes, "I have learned to be content whatever the circumstances. I know what it is to be in need, and I know what it is to have plenty. I have learned the secret of being content in any and every situation, whether well fed or hungry, whether living in plenty or in want."[6]

Paul emphasized the importance of contentment on two occasions (see Philippians 4 and 1 Timothy 6). Yet somewhere between his theological teaching and our lifestyle application, a fog rolled in.

WHAT CONTENTMENT IS NOT

In our propensity to get things wrong, we have attributed to contentment attitudes and feelings that have nothing to do with it. Contentment isn't denying one's feelings about unhappiness, but instead a freedom from being controlled by those feelings.

It isn't pretending things are right when they are not, but instead the peace that comes from knowing that God is bigger than any problem and that He works them all out for our good.

Contentment isn't the complacency that defeats any attempt to make things better, but instead the willingness to work tirelessly for improvement, clinging to God rather than results.

It isn't a feeling of well-being contingent on keeping circumstances under control, but instead a joy that exists in spite of circumstances and looks to the God who never varies.

It isn't the comfortable feeling we get when all our needs and desires are met, but instead the security in knowing, as A. W. Tozer reminds us, that "The man who has God for his treasure has all things in One."[7]

Finally, contentment isn't that pseudo-virtue of the "American dream" where we claim solidarity with Paul from the easy chair of middle-class America. We profess to having learned the secret of contentment in all circumstances, yet we've never experienced forty lashes, stoning, shipwreck, hunger, thirst, homelessness, or imprisonment. Perhaps none of us should presume maturity until the truer tests have been endured. To snuggle up alongside Paul and profess contentment without having known want seems a bit impudent on our part. Paul's contentment in need and plenty is mostly of interest because of the need. Until we know true need and survive the test, we must not presume to be his companion.

THE LAST SHALL BE FIRST

I believe Mrs. Nguyen Thi An (a fictitious name) can claim a rightful companionship with Paul. Though she has lost everything, she has all things in One. They have taken her husband, her home, and her belongings, yet her contentment they cannot take.

Mrs. An's husband was a pastor in Vietnam. When their church was closed by police, he was thrown into prison. Without official papers, she and her children were forced to live on a balcony outside an apartment. Yet her faith forged a sanctuary there out of her surroundings, from which she greets us:

> My Dear Friends,
>
> . . . You know around here we are experiencing hardships, but we thank the Lord He is comforting us and caring for us in every way. When we experience misfortune, adversity, distress and hardship, only then do we see the real blessing of the Lord poured down on us in such a way that we cannot contain it.
>
> We have been obliged recently to leave our modest apartment and for over two months have been living on a balcony. The rain has been beating down and soaking us. Sometimes in the middle of the night we are forced to gather our blankets and run to seek refuge in a stairwell.
>
> Do you know what I do then? I laugh and I praise the Lord, because we can still take shelter in the stairwell. I think of how many people are experiencing much worse hardships than I am. Then I remember the words of the Lord, "To the poor, O Lord, You

are a refuge from the storm, a shadow from the heat" (cp. Isaiah 25:4), and I am greatly comforted. . . .

Our Father . . . is the One who according to the Scriptures does not break the bruised reed nor put out the flickering lamp. He is the One who looks after the orphan and the widow. He is the One who brings blessings and peace to numberless people.

I do not know what words to use in order to describe the love that the Lord has shown our family. I only can bow my knee and my heart and offer to the Lord words of deepest thanks and praise. Although we have lost our house and our possessions, we have not lost the Lord, and He is enough. With the Lord I have everything. The only thing I would fear losing is His blessing!

Could I ask you and our friends in the churches abroad to continue to pray for me that I will faithfully follow the Lord and serve Him regardless of what the circumstances may be?

As far as my husband is concerned, I was able to visit him this past summer. We had a 20-minute conversation that brought us great joy. . . .

I greet you with my love.

Mrs. Nguyen Thi An[8]

Would that she could finish this chapter, and I could be her student.

THE RELENTLESS POWER OF DISCONTENT

Despite her impoverished circumstances, Mrs. Nguyen Thi An races far ahead of affluent America. Why is contentment so hard for us? For one thing, it's slippery. Contentment is not at all like cutting down a tree, which, when it is done, is done. It's more like trying to pick up mercury with tweezers — it keeps squirting away. It's like the carrot suspended two feet in front of our face that moves every time we do. We keep chasing, and it keeps dodging. "Give a man everything he wants," declared Immanuel Kant, "and at that moment, everything will not be everything."

Beyond its slippery nature, contentment is difficult to achieve because of the relentless power of discontent. The battle waged between contentment and discontent is often subtle but never soft. When we enter the material world for our contentment, it pulls us in deeper and deeper, and the pull is deceptively strong. That for which I long becomes that to which I belong.

In addition, contentment is difficult because it is a relative state—at least the world's practice of it is relative. A number of factors influence this relativism: the age in which we live, the local culture, and the lifestyle of family members and friends. If you live in New York City and all your neighbors drive Mercedes, you might feel embarrassed if you drive a pickup. Living in rural Wisconsin where many people cut firewood, however, you would find an older truck more acceptable.

If we were to draw one line representing ALL THERE IS TO HAVE and another representing WHAT WE NOW HAVE, the gap between these lines would be, in most cases, proportional to our level of contentment.

ALL THERE IS TO HAVE

(education, looks, money,
job, marriage, family,
house, cars, toys,
prestige, power, friends,
athleticism, etc.)

WHAT WE NOW HAVE

As the top line rises, the gap between what we now have and all there is to have becomes greater. Often our discontent becomes greater as well. One of the dubious advantages progress has given us is the relentless raising of the top line. Progress perceives this as its duty—to give us more and more. Were we free to select among the opportunities without pressure or comparison, perhaps these abundant choices would be acceptable. But humans are not like that, or at least our society is not like that. Life in the United States has become essentially a comparative experience.

With the invention of air conditioning, for example, progress raised the top line. Before the arrival of air conditioning, no one was discontented to drive in sweltering heat without it. People were miserable because of the heat, perhaps, but not discontented, because you cannot be discontented about something that doesn't exist. Yet when progress invents it for us, the level of expectation rises, and with it the level of discontent.

Living in Texas without an air-conditioned car today, you would likely be discontented. Fifty years ago you would not have been. Some might retort, "Before air conditioning people were miserable, and now, some are discontented. Isn't it about the same?" No. To be miserable with the heat is not a sin.

SET-POINTS

The relativism of contentment can be illustrated using the concept of a "floating set-point." This set-point, somewhat different for each person, is positioned at that level where you are content. If your circumstances match this set-point, you are temporarily satisfied. Once additional possibilities enter your awareness, however, your set-point floats up to a new level. Then you buy a bigger house, get a better-paying job, move south, or undertake a multitude of other "improvements," and again you are temporarily satisfied.

This contentment set-point is free to float upward without limitation. There is no apparent ceiling, and we have not tried to establish one as a matter of public policy, let alone common sense. Instead, we have fueled our economy by stimulating the set-point to rise even faster than it normally would. While this set-point is free-floating, it moves almost always in the upward direction. To see it fall voluntarily in a person's life is a wondrous thing, almost miraculous; I might even say, suggestive of godliness.

The Prosperity Ladder

Another erroneous measure of contentment is the prosperity ladder. Most of us look "up the ladder" and notice that the wealthy have more than we do. This, of course, strikes a near fatal blow at one's contentment. If, instead, we reversed our gaze and looked down the ladder, our gratitude would thrive and opportunities for sharing would abound.

The pettiness of my own sources of discontent would be amusing were I not so repentant about them. I have been known to grumble when our house temperature drops to sixty degrees, yet there are untold millions in the world who do not have shelter. I have been known to complain if the day is rainy, yet a large segment of the world's land is shriveling up in drought. I have been known to groan if I miss my dinner, yet thousands who go to sleep tonight without food will not awaken in the morning.

This relativism, where the grass is greener on your neighbor's lawn, can be remedied, but first it must be confessed. We need to quit staring at those who have more than we do. We need to override the set-point by spiritual maturity, to look down rather than up the ladder, and to fix our contentment on godliness rather than relativism. It helps immeasurably if we are surrounded by a community of like-minded friends rather than a society where envy has been normalized.

The normalization of envy is yet another reason why the achievement of contentment is difficult. Ours has been called "the age of envy." The cultural message is strong: Why shouldn't we want what others have? We have rights, including the right to enjoy the good life. This, of course, is precisely the kind of logic that destroys not only contentment but margin as well.

Manufactured Need

The advertising industry, at $250 billion a year, deserves a great share of the blame for consciously stimulating a chronic state of discontent by continually convincing us that *more* and *better* is desirable. Somehow in the process we forgot scriptural admonitions. I am not aware of a single person who takes seriously these words of Paul at their deepest level: "If we have food and clothing, we will be content with that."[9]

Two broad types of advertising deserve mentioning. The first reminds or informs: "We are having a sale this week," or "When looking for good fried chicken, we serve nightly until 9:00 PM." The second type of advertising stimulates or manipulates need: "All the best athletes use Ajax breath mints," or "Use Jake's new and improved fishing lure and you will never have another boring minute of fishing." Nearly every advertisement that interrupts my consciousness (I do not seek them out—they trespass) is of the latter type.

At first, the lying was subtle, and we overlooked it. Then it became progressively more blatant, wrapped in entertainment. Today, the lying is at absurd levels but goes largely unnoticed. Thus we have the intentional stimulation of covetousness through the telling of shameless lies, both of which Scripture condemns. Yet we sit in rapt attention.

The advertisers use many additional strategies—visual stimulation and sexual innuendo are but two of the more prominent—yet all these are methods. What we really need to understand is the message. My point is, the message we are given is that we need something. That we really do not need much at all is viewed by advertisers as an obstacle to overcome. They must manufacture need.

If we actually needed the thing, advertisers would not have to convince us of it. "The fact that wants can be synthesized by advertising, catalyzed by salesmanship, and shaped by the discreet manipulations of the persuaders shows that they are not very urgent," notes economist John Kenneth Galbraith. "A man who is hungry need never be told of his need for food."[10] We are not a hungry society; we are, in reality, overfed. Need must be created, and discontent must be stirred up.

POISON VERSUS PEACE

These manufacturers of need have been eminently successful, which has been helpful for the economy but troublesome for veracity. In truth, discontent has so many disadvantages one wonders why it is popular. It can suffocate freedom, leaving us in bondage to our desires. It can poison relationships with jealousy and competition. It often rewards blessing with ingratitude as we grumble against God. "Discontent will destroy your peace, rob you of joy, make you miserable, spoil your witness," warns J. I. Packer. "We dishonor God if we proclaim a Savior who satisfies and then go around discontent."[11] And when it has done its work, discontent abandons us, leaving us no comfort in our indebted, marginless, friendless self-pity.

The advantages of contentment, on the other hand, are many: freedom, gratitude, rest, peace—all components of health. They who are content do not have to worry about the latest styles or what to wear tomorrow. They can rejoice in their neighbor's good fortune without having to feel inferior. They do not fret with wrinkles or graying because they accept what comes. They do not have to worry how they might buy this or that because they have no desire for this or that. They are not consumed with how to get out of debt because they have no debt. They have time for gratitude even in small things. They have time for relationships because possessions and the bank do not own them.

Do you see how a life of contentment both enables and supports margin? And do you see how a life filled with contentment and margin both enables and supports healthy relationships?

CONTENTMENT AND RELATIONSHIPS

God commanded contentment because He knew we would need it to anchor right relationships.

We relate better to God when we are satisfied with what He gives. We might say words of worship, but if our heart is not resting in the contentment of His presence, He is not fooled. "The Christian position from the beginning," contends historian Herbert Schlossberg, "has been that people are satisfied by becoming reconciled with God, not by acquiring wealth."[12]

We relate better to self when contented with our circumstances. If allowed to write a prescription redesigning our body, personality, or station in life, most of us would grab at the chance: smarter, funnier, richer, better looking, taller, thinner, more athletic. Yet none of these requests would even be an issue were it not for our comparisons with others. If we were all alone with God (which, in regard to contentment, we are), we would have a different set of values than the one society offers.

We relate better to others when the relationship is stabilized by contentment. If every encounter with my neighbor reminds me of something I covet, that relationship becomes tenuous. Envy makes it hard to have friends—everyone I know has something I do not.

CONTENTMENT AND MONEY

Our relationship to money is another area where contentment is essential. The poor envy the rich, while the rich envy the richer. Money gives a thrill but no satiety. The rich soon sense this and are perhaps surprised by it, but then go back to making more money anyway. Satisfaction will come later, they speculate, and if it never comes, at least there is the thrill.

Money does seem to meet our needs in the short term. It buys us food, shelter, vehicles, and experiences. It does not, however, meet any of our deeper long-term needs: love, truth, relationship, redemption. This short-term deception is difficult for us to understand and is one of the reasons God spent so much time instructing us concerning money and wealth. Money is treacherous, we are told, and riches are deceitful. It is not a sin to be wealthy, but it can be dangerous. "God is merciful and can deliver the rich from the danger of being rich," observes John White. "But many of us do not want to be delivered."[13]

Many of today's rich are faced with the same depression, meaninglessness, alcoholism, suicide, and fractured relationships we see in the poor (or, for that matter, the middle class). The poor are not surprised by their plight. The rich, however, have run the rainbow out to its end and have found it an unexpectedly empty journey.

"To Americans usually tragedy is wanting something very badly and not getting it," observed Henry Kissinger. "Many people have had to learn in their private lives, and nations have had to learn in their historical experience, that perhaps the worst form of tragedy is wanting something badly, getting it, and finding it empty."[14]

Millions, as Kissinger hints, have had to discover that they can't find true contentment in important jobs and that the advertised contentment of cars, houses, and wardrobes is but a short-term hoax. The things one can buy with money are never the things that last. "Keep your lives free from the love of money and be content with what you have," we read in Hebrews, "because God has said, 'Never will I leave you; never will I forsake you.'"[15]

Did your car or your house ever say, "Never will I leave you"? I heard of a million-dollar house that burned to the ground in ten minutes.

While earning money is obviously necessary at some level, the apostle Paul taught that seeking wealth would threaten us with devastation. Paul wrote in 1 Timothy 6:9-10 that people who want to get rich:

- Fall into temptation.
- Fall into a trap.
- Fall into foolish desires.
- Fall into harmful desires.
- Are plunged into ruin.
- Are plunged into destruction.

And some people eager for money:

- Have wandered from the faith.
- Have pierced themselves with many griefs.

Do you want to be plunged and pierced? Nor do I. But that doesn't seem to stop us from wanting to get rich. Were Paul's message not included in the biblical text, it would be out of print. No readership remains, even within the church.

The Theology of Enough

We need contentment to relate correctly to money and, in a similar way, to possessions. The rules here are simple:

1. God comes first and possessions come second.
2. Possessions are to be used, not loved.

One of Jesus' most vivid warnings to contemporary America is His rebuke of the rich landowner in Luke 12. When the fields yielded a great harvest, the landowner proudly built huge barns and stored up his treasure for the years to come. Now, he thought, life will be easy and secure.

God's judgment was quick: "You fool!" That night the man's life was taken from him.

"Watch out!" warns Jesus. "Be on your guard against all kinds of greed; a man's life does not consist in the abundance of his possessions" (Luke 12:15). Tragically, for many of us today, our lives do indeed consist in the abundance of our possessions.

"Within the human heart 'things' have taken over," asserts A. W. Tozer. "God's gifts now take the place of God, and the whole course of nature is upset by the monstrous substitution."[16] Why hasn't the Church stood against this popular error? Why hasn't there been a clear expression of a "theology of enough"? Perhaps it is because things are not evil, as stealing and adultery are; only the love of things, like the love of money, is evil. It is easy for us to say, "I don't love this thing; it's just that I need it." God is what we need; things are what we use. In the words of one Christian journalist, "Contentment lies not in what is yours, but in whose you are."[17]

Boredom and Suffering

Contentment is also helpful in enduring boredom and suffering. Children today use the word *boring* frequently. It is intended as the ultimate verbal scourge, and basically it means, "I'm discontented. Entertain me." The prevalence of this word is an unsettling indicator of where our children are in relation to contentment.

As I was growing up, we used our imagination and creativity to make our own fun. Today, electronic entertainment rides a nonstop conveyer belt directly into the dormant souls of the young. It is not a favorable development. I cannot be optimistic that this trend will miraculously result in a mature sense of contentment in later years. Over time, a fallen log will not turn into a house. All you get is a bigger pile of decay.

> A man said to the universe:
> "Sir, I exist!"
>> "However," replied the universe,
>> "The fact has not created in me
>> A sense of obligation."[18]

In his famous poem, Stephen Crane reminds us of an important truth: God is not indebted to us. If life is boring, then it is boring. We work to make it better, but our duty throughout the working is contentment. If life is tough, so it is tough. Our duty is contentment. If there is suffering, why would we expect anything different? Our duty is contentment.

Life can be painful. Most people do not choose this pain; it comes with living. Contentment, however, is different. Contentment or discontent is a matter of the will, a choice. When we choose obedience, God, in His wonderful way with surprises, can redeem the pain and suffering in our lives and can turn the destruction into benefit.

DON'T WAIT—WORK

No formula exists for finding contentment other than obedience. Remember, it is a secret. First you must seek it: then it will be revealed to you. It won't make sense to worldly thinking, and it won't be discovered by scientific study. First you must seek it. Then it will be revealed to you.

This, of course, is no excuse to sit around waiting to hear from heaven.

There are steps you can take, acts of your will, that point you in the right direction. You always have a better chance of discovering the secret if you're in the vicinity of its hiding place. The following steps will start you on your way.

1. Get to work. The conflict between contentment and discontent is a struggle format and requires effort on our part. You cannot get from New Orleans to Minneapolis on the Mississippi except by paddling.

2. Divorce your thinking from society's relativistic standards. God says, "Be content," not "Be content if . . ." Never allow the affairs of others to influence your contentment.

3. Turn off the ads. If you wish to preserve your financial margin, cast your lot with contentment.

4. Defer to God's opinion concerning your family relationships. How often, particularly in modern America, have we seen the devastation visited upon families through the "if only" syndrome? Emotional margin is an early casualty with such discontent as, "If only my wife were more appealing or more sexually interested," or "If only my husband made more money or had more hair." Infidelity, even in thought, is greener grass only because it's been spray painted by the Deceiver himself. Contentment keeps our eyes on the right side of the fence.

5. Set new standards for contentment using the truth of Scripture. God has long desired to teach us these principles, but it has not been an easy task for Him.

6. Develop "counter-habits," as John Charles Cooper calls them. Instead of getting, try giving. Instead of replacing, try preserving. Instead of feeling covetous, try feeling grateful. Instead of feeling inferior before men, try feeling accepted before God. Instead of being ruled by feelings, try enjoying the freedom of contentment.

7. Subtract from your needs. Make a list of all the things you need and then start crossing things off. It might at first be painful, but after a while it becomes fun. "There are two ways to get enough,"

G. K. Chesterton has pointed out. "One is to continue to accumulate more and more. The other is to desire less."

8. Accept from God's hand that which He gives—not resignation, not complacency, but contentment. All that is needful He will supply. Even pain and suffering that seemingly cannot be corrected, He can redeem.

9. If you still do not feel the stirrings of contentment within, argue with yourself and tell yourself the truth. We discover contentment, according to Packer, "by learning to talk to ourselves in a good Christian way. You listen to God in Scripture and then tell yourself what He said. If your emotions disagree, you argue with your emotions. And if you find unbelief in your heart, you argue with that unbelief and drive it out by appeal to God's truth."[19]

DISLOCATION OR DELIGHT?

Is contentment, then, a move in the health direction? Let's ask the masters, advising us from the seventeenth century.

"Discontent doth dislocate and unjoint the soul, it pulls off the wheels," advises Thomas Watson in *The Art of Divine Contentment*. "Discontent is a fretting humour, which dries the brains, wastes the spirits, corrodes and eats out the comfort of life."[20]

On the other hand, writes Jeremiah Burroughs in *The Rare Jewel of Christian Contentment*, "Christian contentment is that sweet, inward, quiet, gracious frame of spirit, which freely submits to and delights in God's wise and fatherly disposal in every condition."[21]

When I get sick, I want to go to their clinic. They never knew about penicillin. But they sure knew a lot about health.

HEALTH THROUGH SIMPLICITY

THOUGH IT HAS been variously commended and practiced for centuries, simplicity has seldom been more needed than it is today. Health requires it. Sanity demands it. Contentment facilitates it.

If overload is sabotaging our equilibrium, simplicity can help. If we find ourselves being detailed to death, simplicity can restore life. If we find ourselves overextended in our emotional, financial, and time commitments, simplicity is one of the best ways to reestablish margin.

GETTING AWAY FROM IT ALL

We hear frequent talk about the rat race and the treadmill, about stopping the world to let people off. Many fantasize about walking away from their jobs, throwing away the television, and moving to a cabin in the woods. Indeed, in the last few decades, many have acted upon the fantasy.

Given the complicated, rushed nature of daily life, it is not surprising that many are looking for the exit door. The solution, however, for our stress-overload-complexity triad is not so much escaping as it is transcending: The solution is simplicity. Simplicity does not guarantee margin, but it is at least a step in the right direction.

NOT A MODERN INVENTION

In our age of frenzied distress, large numbers of contemporary thinkers have begun discussing and writing about the concept of a simple lifestyle. We encounter with regularity such phrases as "the plain life," "plain people," "intermediate technology," "intentional communities," and "contrast culture." We are enamored by the Amish, wanting to tour their villages and bring home their quilts. Even the popular "country look" in home decorating has become a manifestation of the nostalgia many share about things simple and past.

Despite its attractiveness and timeliness, simplicity is not a new concept. The spiritually minded have long sought it as a way of facilitating the contemplative life. The monastic orders and the Desert Fathers practiced simplicity, often including vows of poverty, asceticism, and separation from the world.

Through the seventeenth and eighteenth centuries, many who traveled to the New World in search of religious freedom, from the Puritans to the Quakers, sought a simple, godly lifestyle. America of the nineteenth century also saw its simplicity movements. Perhaps the most lasting impressions were made by the Transcendentalists, a group who were in many ways spiritually motivated but not within the context of orthodox Christian doctrine. Two of their number, Ralph Waldo Emerson and Henry David Thoreau, were articulate prophets for this "plain living and high thinking," and their legacy continues to influence many today.

The modern era has witnessed such simplicity causes as the hippie communes and cultural dropouts. In addition, there has been significant activity within the Church, although not always mainstream. From the International Consultation of Simple Life-Style to the Mennonite Central Committee, some in the Church seek to find the posture of proper theological balance in an age of affluence and complexity.

Austere separatists such as the Amish, once widely scorned for being so backward, now garner more respect. "We should look again at the life styles and beliefs of the Brethren, Mennonites, and Amish," encourages author John Charles Cooper. "They do not pollute the earth. They do not waste food. They concentrate on the care of the earth and the care of their families. They have no ambitions for wealth or status. They harbor no political lusts to control the lives of their neighbors. All they ask for is the right to live simple, godly lives. The joy of these plain people lies in their communion with Christ and with one another."[1]

CHRISTLIKENESS

Even if I were not a Christian, the notion of stepping off the treadmill would sound attractive. Yet for adherents of Christianity, a stronger pull motivates: To be a follower of Christ means we should *follow* Him. No one lived a simpler, more unencumbered life than He. His birth was spartan, and His life was free from the ties of possessions or money. He was born with nothing, lived with little, and died with nothing. His simplicity was not accidental. Jesus could have chosen any standard, yet He chose to live simply.

In the Sermon on the Mount, Christ told us not to worry even about food and clothing and not to worry about tomorrow. That He did not seek luxury is a statement to us who follow Him. When He demonstrated servitude by washing the feet of His disciples, He explained, "I have set you an example that you should do as I have done for you. . . . No servant is greater than his master."[2]

The apostle Peter instructs us to walk after the example of Christ in enduring suffering.[3] Paul teaches us to follow after Jesus' example of humility.[4] "Does the Bible infer that we are to live like *a king* or like *the King*?" asks Rev. Tom Allen. "The simplicity, sacrifice and servanthood of Jesus Christ should be our way of life, too."[5]

INTERNAL ANCHOR, EXTERNAL JOY

All external manifestations of the Christian life require internal foundations, and simplicity is no different. The external practices are important, but the internal requirements are essential. For simplicity to bring us the rest we need, the internal truths must be confirmed by our own will. They have to do with the lordship of Christ. This means seeking the kingdom first, thus giving over our plans, our expectations, our future, our family, our reputation, and our possessions to Him. Once these conditions are met, then we are free to begin seeking the external practices.

With the internal issues settled, the external practices are a joy. Loaning or giving away possessions is not anxiety-producing because we are only stewards anyway, and the true Owner has told us to give generously. We are free to wear older clothes or to live in modest homes because God doesn't care. We no longer need to impress. With the internal truth anchored, the external simplicity is a celebration. Without this anchor, however, the external workings become a chore, a set of rules, and often degenerate into legalism.

WHAT IT IS

Simple living over the centuries has been variously defined. "The precise meaning of the simple life has never been fixed," explains historian David Shi. "Rather, it has always represented a shifting cluster of ideas, sentiments, and activities."[6] Certain common threads, however, can be identified. The simple life is:

Voluntary—If the simple life is forced, it ceases to be simple. Involuntary impoverishment, for example, makes it difficult for people to choose simplicity. The plain life is far more profitable when it is chosen as an act of the will.

Free—One of the key features of simplicity and, at the same time, one of its principal advantages is that it is a life of freedom. It is free from anxiety—about our reputations, our possessions, our tomorrows. It is being controlled by that which is life-giving and refusing to be controlled by that which is destructive.

Uncluttered—Realizing that psychological and material clutter impedes our journey, simplicity seeks to unclutter. Emotionally, we release our worries, we reconcile our relationships, we forgive our enemies, and we begin anew each day. Materially, instead of possession gluttony, we practice de-accumulation. Like runners of old, we strip down to that which is authentic so that we might run the race effectively.

Natural—We respect the natural order—the things God has created and the job God has given humankind within that order. We don't just return to nature; we return to the God who created nature. The simple life understands that natural beauty exists and that it penetrates deeper than the adornments of humankind. The real beauty of another human exists within the spirit and consists of virtue and purity.

Creative—Life is not boring just because it is simple. Simplicity sets the imagination free to work and to enjoy. Passive entertainment can dull the sense of wonder God has placed within us. The simple life, however, affords an opportunity to rediscover the joys of creativity.

Authentic—A simple lifestyle must distinguish between the spiritually authentic and spiritually inauthentic aspects of life and be devoted to the former. Biblical authenticity includes those things God has told us to focus on, those things that have eternal, God-assigned value: people, love, service, worship, prayer, self-denial, relationships, contentment, freedom, rest.

Focused—Understanding the significance of spiritual authenticity, we focus on it. We lock in on what is good and true and eternal. This does not mean we don't wash our car or take out the garbage. But it does mean that we understand who God is and what His priorities for our lives are—and then follow them. It does mean that we focus intensely on seeking first the kingdom and on loving God and man. Without such focus, we drift.

Margined—Simplicity recognizes the importance of margin and seeks to protect it. Together margin and simplicity are allies in a hostile world. Like a team of oxen straining against the storm, they will not be beaten back by the forces that seek to crush them both. The pace might plod. But they are a reliable team, always pulling together. Given time, the work will get done. Thanks to their efforts, relational and spiritual health have a better chance.

Disciplined—Restraint is necessary for successful living, and all the more for simple living. Comfort is not a legitimate primary goal—authenticity is. Understandably, then, those seeking simplicity may experience discomfort. Doing without is often necessary. Inasmuch as the simple life is an obedient life, and obedience requires discipline, we will not be able to thrive without it.

Diligent—The simple life knows how to rest, but it also knows how to work. One of the benefits of simplicity is a return to human labor. It is time to rethink the notion that small-scale, labor-intensive production is undesirable. It is good to be physically active and to work with our hands. It is good to start and end the work ourselves and to have pride in the process and the product. It is good to plant our own food, to sew our own clothes, to cut our own wood, to walk to work.

Healthful—A life voluntarily chosen and lived in freedom; a life uncluttered and natural; a life that is focused, diligent, and disciplined; a life characterized by creativity and spiritual authenticity—is not this a healthy life?

WHAT SIMPLICITY ISN'T

Misconceptions abound about the simple life. We can clarify simplicity as much by explaining what it isn't as by delineating what it is. And it is not:

Easy—Many equate "simple" with "easy" and become disillusioned with simple living when they find out how hard it can be. To bake your own bread or cut your own wood is not always the easiest way to provide food and warmth. But doing these chores yourself allows an often hardearned independence that can facilitate simplicity.

Legalistic—Legalism is the trap I dread more than any other. Those who choose to live a simple lifestyle often set a standard of judgment for the lives of others. Such legalism does not liberate; it kills. It destroys the joy of both the accuser and the accused. The message of simple living is better spread by invitation than by judgment.

Proud—While simple living is intended to be a vehicle for virtue, it can deteriorate into the vice of pride. This we might call "reverse pride." It is possible, and sometimes even tempting, to wear patches on your clothes as self-awarded badges of righteousness. It is possible to practice self-exaltation for the rust on your car or the stone-ground whole-wheat bread in your oven. All of these highly visible "sacrifices" serve to elevate your (perceived) righteousness level several notches above that of your inferiors. Jesus dealt with this prideful attitude in the Sermon on the Mount, and no new teaching is needed.

Impoverished—Taking a vow of poverty does not guarantee that spiritually authentic simplicity will follow. Simplicity does not reject money and ownership—it merely subjugates it. All money goes quickly to the purse of the Father for use in our lives and the lives of others according to His wishes. We don't seek wealth as a goal in itself, not only because it is sinful to do so, but also because money cannot buy what we need. Yet money is received and used, for the Father knows how to control it for the purposes of His kingdom.

Ascetic—Asceticism rejects all possessions and argues that "things" are spiritually handicapping. While it is true that things can become spiritually inauthentic, they are not an *a priori* evil. God is a good Creator, and He has created a whole world full of good things. It is not wrong to use them—they were made to be used. But our material appetites must be controlled.

Neurotic—Some adherents live a simple life but know nothing of its freedom. They tilt toward spartan asceticism because they feel unworthy of any blessing or they feel responsible for all the poverty in the world. Such a guilt-driven lifestyle is not simplicity. It is neurosis. God blames us only for what we are to blame for, and He took it all away when we asked Him to. Now that the slate is clean, we choose simplicity, not out of guilt but out of sensitivity and devotion.

Ignorant—Simple livers are not to be simpletons. We don't achieve such a lifestyle by burning our books and burying our heads. On the contrary, one of the main advantages of such a life is the opportunity it provides for study, discussion, and meditation. God created our brains just as surely as He did our hearts, and He expects us to use them both for His glory. Ignorance is not the essence of simplicity—it is an enemy.

Escapist—"The grass is greener on the other side of the fence" is 98 percent lie. We don't attain the simple life by throwing away our cars and phones and running off to live in the woods. Clearly, for some people the simple life is facilitated by moving from an overmortgaged house or departing a traffic-paralyzed city. But simple living is not a location; it is an attitude. It is not escaping; it is transcending. It is not separation; it is sanctification.

A RETREAT TO THE PAST?

Many among us might wish to turn back the clock, to retreat to a simpler, easier time. We long for the quiet of nature rather than the blast of rock music and car horns. We want to be more directly involved in the elements, whether planting the seed that feeds our family or digging the worms that catch our fish. Perhaps we even long to raise our own animals or build our own log home.

Much debate continues over such nostalgia. Is it healthy or is it escapist? Is sentimentality an ally or a deceiver? We often forget the horrid problems of the past, and in the process, also overlook the blessings of today. Our historical memories are selective. To pine for a misrepresented dreamland is not a spiritually authentic thing to do.

In addition to calling such nostalgia irresponsible, some argue we could not reverse the process of history even if we wanted to. "We can't turn back the clock" they insist. When Art Gish was confronted with the question of turning back the clock, his answer was enlightening: "The analogy of a clock is not helpful. It is not the question of a clock, but a compass. The issue is not chronology, but direction. And that we can decide. . . . We are not retreating, but looking ahead to perceive what is important. Simplification implies leaving things behind and moving to a new future."[7]

THE DIFFICULTY OF SIMPLICITY

What factors make the simple life hard to obtain? If we embark on this journey, let's first decide how much fortitude we need to bring with us.

No sooner have we started out the gate then we encounter our first problem: *society's disrespect*. If we choose to ignore fashion and status, we will not gain the admiration of our peers. From the outset, we need to decide who it is we are trying to please. And why.

Continuing down the narrow road of the simple life, we keep encountering another problem: *our own expectations*. After decades of convenience and affluence, we not only desire but expect ease and satiation. Gratification of our appetites has become a widespread goal not seriously challenged by the Church. If we do not reprogram such expectations, we will experience recurrent frustration in our search for simplicity.

Our lack of discipline presents us with yet another obstacle. We have not needed much discipline during this era of abundance, and we have lost interest in it as a component of lifestyle. Most of us have grown soft. But the simple life is not easy, and discipline is necessary.

Finally, *our own mistaken opinions* of how things ought to be also trip us repeatedly. Theological confusion has permitted us first to look at what we want and then to build a theology that justifies it. Instead, we need to judge our opinions repeatedly with the truth of Scriptures.

SUGGESTIONS

The following are suggestions that will assist in simple living. Beware of the distinction between suggestions and rules, for if you make them rules, you will have converted simplicity into legalism and defeated its purpose before even beginning.

Possessions and Finances
- Cultivate contentment, desire less.
- Resist covetousness.
- Resist consumerism.
- Wage war against advertisements.
- Buy things for their usefulness rather than their status.
- De-accumulate.

- Develop the habit of giving away.
- Share possessions.
- Offer the use of your possessions—don't make others ask.
- Develop a network of exchange.
- Avoid overindulging—for example, toys, food, movie viewing, etc.
- Avoid impulse buying.
- Don't buy anything if the time and money spent on it compete with family, service, and God.
- Avoid debt if possible.
- Don't buy now, pay later.
- Avoid credit cards if they are a problem.
- Reject fashion, especially fads.
- De-emphasize respectability.
- Simplify your wardrobe—give away excess.
- Learn how to make do with a lower income instead of needing a higher one.

Pace and Atmosphere

- Slow down.
- Do not exhaust your emotional bank account.
- Lie fallow.
- Say no.
- Enjoy peaceful music.
- Control/restrict/eliminate television watching; surfing the net.
- Get a remote control and turn off advertisements.

Relationships

- Cultivate a closeness with God.
- Schedule "simple" dates with your spouse.
- Teach your children.
- Enjoy family field trips.
- Practice regular hospitality.
- Help each other, emphasize service.
- Encourage others.

- "Always speak the truth and you'll never be concerned with your memory."
- Don't judge.
- Learn to enjoy solitude.

Appreciation

- Send cards of encouragement and appreciation when others are not expecting it.
- Be grateful for things large and small.
- Emphasize a joyful life.
- Appreciate creation.

Spiritual Life

- Make the Word central.
- Meditate, memorize.
- Pray.
- Encourage simple worship.

Activities

- Make your commitments simple.
- Don't overwork.
- Fast periodically from media, food, people.
- Elevate reading, go to the library.
- Simplify Christmas.
- Write down those things you need to remember and forget everything else.

Nutrition and Exercise

- Exercise.
- Bike or walk.
- Make your recreation active rather than passive.
- Develop healthy sleep habits.
- Avoid overeating.
- Frequent a co-op.

- Whenever possible, buy food directly from those who grow it.
- Garden.

Fad or the Future?

Is simplicity a trendy fad? Will it fade in significance as did the communes, or is it destined to grow in importance? Simple lifestyles, or something approximating that idea, will only continue to increase in importance. Our age is becoming more complex and diffusely overloaded, and simplicity is a movement whose time has come.

One hundred years ago, the most popular spokesman for simple living was the writer John Burroughs. Naturalists and students, journalists and politicians (including Theodore Roosevelt) wore a path to the door of his rustic New England cabin. Humble and self-effacing, he was an eloquent spokesman for unencumbered living. He said:

> I am bound to praise the simple life because I have lived it and found it good. When I depart from it, evil results follow. I love a small house, plain clothes, simple living. . . . To see the fire that warms you, or better yet, to cut the wood that feeds the fire that warms you; to see the spring where the water bubbles up that slakes your thirst, and to dip your pail into it; . . . to be in direct and personal contact with the sources of your material life; to want no extras, no shields; to find the universal elements enough . . . to be thrilled by the stars at night; to be elated over a bird's nest, or over a wild flower in spring—these are some of the rewards of the simple life.[8]

Do these strike you as sentiments that future generations will scoff at—or yearn for?

I agree.

WHAT DOES THE LORD REQUIRE?

The simple life sounds all the more attractive when you are in love with the Truth. If you have such a love, anything that distracts you from Truth is gladly cut adrift. Then, after you have been freed to pursue your path unencumbered, you will not desire more from your days on earth than simply to act justly, to love mercy, and to walk humbly with your God.[9]

HEALTH THROUGH BALANCE

The human body is a universe. Made up of 10^{28} atoms, we each contain millions of times more atoms than there are stars in space. Ninety percent of these atoms are replaced every year, and virtually 100 percent are replaced every five years. Thus our physical beings are continuously tearing down but also continuously building up. From dust we have come and to dust we return—continuously.[1]

Veritable factories that never shut down, our bodies exhibit a complexity beyond human comprehension. We each are made up of trillions upon trillions of working units, all perpetually moving, metabolizing, combining, interacting, adjusting, purifying, purging, building, and decaying. Yet everything must function in balance. If this balance is disturbed, disease is the result. We get sick. We feel pain.

When organ systems are functioning in a balanced manner, physicians say they are "compensated." To be decompensated—that is, out of balance—is to be ill. Likewise, in the area of mental health, when someone is functioning poorly, he or she is said to be "unbalanced." For physiology to avoid becoming pathology, balance is essential. It is no different in the broader context of life.

The Balancing Act

The balanced life today seems inaccessible: too many activities, too many choices, too many decisions, too many commitments, too many expectations, too many people, too much hurry, too much change. Overload, stress, complexity—all are unbalancing pressures. Their effect is to cause ever-increasing disequilibrium in systems and people.

The average conscientious American wants to be committed as a spouse, responsible as a parent, faithful in the church, successful in the workplace, and active in the community. Family, church, community, self—each one is a legitimate pull. Indeed, life is full of tugs:

Work	Leisure
Action	Meditation
Leading	Following
Speaking	Listening
Handwork	Headwork
Productivity	Recreation
Intensity	Idleness
Serving	Waiting
Giving	Receiving
Applying	Learning
Structure	Spontaneity
Assertiveness	Submissiveness
Confidence	Humility
Judgment	Grace
Analysis	Synthesis
Specialization	Integration
Society	Solitude
Laughter	Solemnity
Duty	Freedom
Joy	Sorrow
External life	Internal life

How does one find the balance? When life is so correctly constituted of both sides, by what criteria do we make decisions? Is balance possible?

Are we to pray or to serve? To work or to rest? To rejoice at the goodness in people and the great goodness in our Creator or to sorrow at the pain so evident all around? Life requires both. Balance has always been necessary and will always be necessary. It is just becoming more difficult.

BALANCE OR EXCELLENCE?

Much is made today of the virtues of excellence. But what does this mean? Often the excellence described is only in one narrow corridor of life: virtuosos who exist only for their music, or corporate executives who live at the office.

What do these passionate high achievers think of balance? For many, it is an enemy. Single-minded fervency is their standard. One-hundred-percent effort is the minimum, and those who question such asymmetrical dedication are distrusted and unpromoted.

While undivided devotion to one cause can bring great success and vault a person into prominence, such a priority structure often leaves the rest of that person's life in a state of disorder. Thus it is not uncommon to discover a physician who fails as a parent, an entertainer who fails as a spouse, a pastor who neglects personal health, or an executive who fails at all those other areas. Traditional wisdom has told us not to put all our eggs in one basket. Yet, in pursuit of excellence, we often discard this basic wisdom. Balance is not the goal; preeminence is the goal.

I'm not advocating halfheartedness and mediocrity, for we should always do our best. But "doing our best" has limits. Our rush toward excellence in one quadrant of life must not be permitted to cause destruction in another. "We need," said Norman Cousins, "to be more proportionate."

Those who go all out for success in one endeavor, points out physicist/engineer Richard H. Bube, risk failure in other important areas of life. "Not only is the ability to exhibit excellence in other fields decreased, but in several fields the net consequence is to produce what we may colloquially call 'negative excellence.'" Bube recommends "a more balanced approach."[2] This principle is demonstrated in figures 13.1 and 13.2 (adapted from Bube).

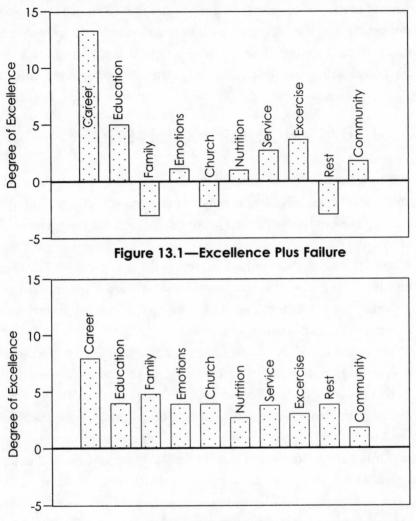

Figure 13.1—Excellence Plus Failure

Figure 13.2–Balance

Schematic illustrations of choice patterns in major fields of a person's endeavors. The ten bars represent individual areas that require time and effort and in which it is possible to establish excellence. (a) This set of choices represents those made by a person who strives for such a high degree of excellence in one area that other areas may actually experience "negative excellence," i.e. failure. (b) This set of choices represents those made by a person who strives to avoid failure in any area and therefore does not achieve quite as high a degree of excellence in any one area as the person represented in (a). Limitations of time and resources make it necessary for every person to choose between some degree of (a) and (b).

The person in figure 13.1 has chosen to strive for such a high degree of excellence in one area that other areas reveal little excellence or even "negative excellence" (that is, failure). Consequently, this person has achieved excellence in the career area but, at the same time, has suffered failure in the other important areas of family, church, and rest.

In contrast, the person in figure 13.2 has chosen to live a balanced life and has therefore avoided "negative excellence" in any area. As a consequence, no outstanding level of excellence has been achieved. On the other hand, no failure has been experienced either.

If you wish to achieve excellence but also to have life balance, beware. Those who advocate excellence at all costs often do not believe in "outside interests" and may not tolerate them. Family, friends, church, as well as margin in personal time and emotional health—all are luxuries that may compete with a stellar performance in a single area. If, then, we are forced to choose between excellence and balance, how do we choose? Once we understand that God expects us to act responsibly in each area of life, it is easier to discern the problems associated with one-track excellence.

A MATTER OF PRIORITIES?

If we accept that balance is important, especially in light of avoiding "negative excellence" in any area of life, how do we achieve it? Since each of us lives according to a set of priorities—whether we are aware of it or not—perhaps that's the place to start.

What does your priority list look like? For those committed to ultra-excellence, one goal stands alone on the top—perhaps wealth, power, athletic success, academics or political victory. Sequentially beneath this exalted goal are myriad subordinate goals. These form a constellation of priorities for each person. If written down, one list might look something like this:

1. God
2. Spouse/marriage

3. Children
4. Self
5. Work
6. Church
7. Friends, neighbors
8. Health
9. Security
10. Civic duty

Does creating such lists help us solve our problem and lead us to biblically authentic decision making about balancing priorities? I think not. "A list of priorities doesn't make sense!" observes J. Grant Howard in *Balancing Life's Demands*. "No matter how you define and describe your particular approach, if it is a sequential approach, it is loaded with contradictions."[3]

We cannot achieve balance by stacking our priorities one on top of another, even though this is a common practice. As Dr. Howard goes on to advise, it fits better to think of God as central to everything and then build outward from that point. We do not love God, then spouse, then children, then self, then church. We love God, spouse, children, self, and church all at the same time. Similarly, we do not love God 100 percent, spouse 95 percent, children 90 percent, church 80 percent. God's standard requires that we love all of them all of the time.

One of the interesting things about love is that it is not a mathematical entity. When divided, love multiplies. However we attempt to factor it, love remains an intact whole. For example, if we have one child in our family, we might be singularly devoted to that child and love him or her 100 percent. If we have a second child, does that mean we love each child only 50 percent? Of course not. We would love each child 100 percent even if there were ten of them.

God has suspended the laws of mathematics in allowing love to expand infinitely. In so doing, He has delivered us from the need to prioritize our love sequentially.

THE APPORTIONMENT OF TIME

It does not make sense to have sequential priorities in terms of love or even in terms of commitment. We love each person fully. Additionally, we are committed to doing good in all areas of life. Priority thinking *is* appropriate, however, when we speak of *time*.

Time is the context within which we all must work. In any given year, no one is granted more time than another person, and no one is granted less. Time cannot be stretched or borrowed. It is a universal given, and it is in apportioning this time that balance and priorities become very important.

Time, then, is the key. When we couple it with our goals, desires, and responsibilities, we have some priority decisions to make. It is unwise to give all our time to work and family, but none to personal health. God created us to need health, and it is not wrong to seek it. Likewise, God created us to need each other in relationship. It is not wrong to dedicate time for that. He created us with duties toward nature, work, and government, and it is not wrong for us to focus on these duties. *But the time devoted must be balanced, for if we give too much in one area we neglect our duty in another important area and fail God's requirements for balanced living.*

RESTORING BALANCE

Partitioning our time is probably the most important practical issue in achieving balanced living. Yet rationing it wisely presents a dilemma for each of us. How do we do it? First and most important, balance cannot be achieved unless we are willing to say No.

It is not easy to say No. Anyone who has eaten in a buffet restaurant knows what it is like to face a long table of inviting foods: salads, potatoes, gravy, rolls, corn, chicken, shrimp, roast beef, and pie. It's difficult to go down this line without saying yes to too much. In life, as in the buffet, our plates fill up sooner than we realize. In attempting to be sociable we try to accommodate everyone's invitations. In attempting to live a full life we taste every experience. In attempting to be good parents we try to give our children more opportunities than we had. In attempting to be compassionate we want to help with everyone's problems. In attempting to be good providers we accept extra work assignments.

At this point we need to remember discussions from earlier in the book. With each passing year, modern-day life spontaneously becomes more stressful, more overloaded, and more complex. No one controls all this change—it is simply the default way progress unfolds. As we are presented with more decision and activity overload within an increasingly complex and stressful context, balance becomes more difficult. We cannot resolve this problem without saying No—even to some very good things. Saying No, then, is the first step. But what comes next?

Following are four additional steps to restoring balance.

1. **Regain control over our own lives.** Only then will balance be a possibility. If our schedules are ruled by the urgent and tyrannical, we will not have the control necessary for substantive changes.

2. **Place God at the center of all things, and build outward from there.** God has told us which areas to focus on—in particular, loving relationships. Making our choices in the light of accepted limits, we reassess regularly and defend each area of importance against the onslaught of other demands.

3. **Beware the trap of trying to solve the problem of imbalance by becoming even more imbalanced.** Sometimes it feels like we are in a Chinese finger trap—the harder we try to pull free, the worse we become entrapped. If already maximally scheduled, we cannot give added attention to one area unless we subtract from another area. "We respond to our sense of imbalance by committing more time and energy to an area in which we feel deficient," warns physician George Rust.[4] Yet when the rain barrel is full, it is full. We cannot put another drop in unless we first take a drop out. As elementary as this principle is, its application escapes the majority of modern-day people.

4. **Accept the No given us by others.** We ought not to feel offended when another person is merely attempting to achieve God-honoring

balance and margin. Let's beware of forcing our expectations upon our friends. Give others the freedom to maneuver within the complicated context of their own lives. If we insist on unbalanced living, at least we should allow those around us to seek balance should they so desire. Even as we reap the rewards for our area of excellence, we will also reap the penalties for the areas of negative excellence. Others might not desire this same scenario.

A FEW SHELLS

One of the most charming books written about balance and simplicity is a small volume by Anne Morrow Lindbergh. Well known as wife of famous pilot Charles Lindbergh and daughter of the diplomat Dwight Morrow, Anne Lindbergh was a celebrity in her own right as aviator and author. Probably her most famous book, *Gift from the Sea*, was written in 1955 during an island retreat off the New England coast. Our personal copy is a 1957 edition, and by that time—two years after first publication—more than one-half million copies had been printed. She wrote:

> For the natural selectivity of the island I will have to substitute a conscious selectivity based on another sense of values—a sense of values I have become more aware of here. Island-precepts, I might call them if I could define them, signposts toward another way of living. Simplicity of living, as much as possible, to retain a true awareness of life. Balance of physical, intellectual, and spiritual life. Work without pressure. Space for significance and beauty. Time for solitude and sharing. Closeness to nature to strengthen understanding and faith in the intermittency of life: life of the spirit, creative life, and the life of human relationships.[5]

GOD UNDERSTANDS

Balance is necessary and attainable—not easy, but possible. When we understand that we are finite and that it is okay to be finite, then we can begin to accept our limits with comfort.

God expects us to perform well in many areas of life. But when He gave us the limits of time and finiteness, at that moment He also built in the necessity of balance. We work hard to please our Master, but we also rest confidently knowing that He understands our condition.

What we do we do well—but we do not do it all.

CHAPTER

14

HEALTH THROUGH REST

THREE-YEAR-OLDS seldom sit still. Bundles of energy tightly wound, they dash from here to there, leaping over toys and ricocheting off walls. Church services were not designed with these squirmers in mind. Each Sunday the rear of the sanctuary witnesses the sixty-minute ritual of parent against child; the one trying to survive, the other trying to escape.

Our eldest son, Adam, was once such a wiggly three-year-old, and I was more than once the embarrassed parent. A particular service stands out vividly. His restless noisiness was not in the least malicious, but it was distracting nevertheless. Attempting to maintain quiet, I lifted him onto my lap and held him loosely in my arms. The wiggling, however, didn't stop. Now, instead of random wiggling, there was willful wiggling. He and I were soon doing battle. Adam was intent on freedom. I was intent on containment.

Finally, after twenty minutes, that blessed moment arrived. As if someone had thrown a switch, he suddenly melted into my arms and fell asleep. The tug of war ended. Adam had yielded and was now at rest. As the struggling ceased, my attitude changed. The frustration of the previous moments vanished, and in its place was a deep protective love. This, I thought, is as it should be — not striving, but nestling. I would have moved mountains at that moment to defend him.

Rest. In the arms of a loving Father.

WEARINESS

The patients who came to my office never seemed rested. For that matter, neither do most physicians. Many people I meet look haggard and worn-out.

Often-used descriptors of our society include active, busy, driven, fatigued, tired, exhausted, weary, burned out, anxious, overloaded, or stressed. But seldom do you hear our society described as "well rested." We are a tired generation, one for which Matthew Arnold's "hurry sickness" has become a way of life. Our carburetors are set on high, and our gears are stuck in overdrive. Our lives are nonstop.

We have leisure but little rest. The pace, the noise, the expectations, and the interruptions of modern life have not soothed the soul nor brought refreshment to the burdened spirit.

FROM JET TO DONKEY

Earlier in the book we took a short trip abroad, visiting Africa and the Caribbean. Let's again pack our bags and head off on another fact-finding mission, this time watching closely for signs of cultural and personal rest-edness. Even though we board a DC-10 in New York, be prepared to dis-embark from the back of a camel in the middle of nowhere.

The first thing we notice is that the pace of life in such places is decid-edly slower than ours. The people have much more time to visit with their neighbors, walk to town, or stop and leisurely watch the children rolling a hoop down the middle of the main street. No one seems in a hurry (except, that is, when they drive).

Just your presence in town brings the entire society to a curious halt. The children flock around and almost all of them are giggling. In the mar-ket, everyone is talking—but only a fraction of the exchange is commer-cial. If you ask for directions, you will have twelve volunteers.

On the main street, men sit on barrel tops and talk. Women lean out of shop windows to visit with the closest passerby. Kids try to hawk their trin-kets or beg for money—but often with the hint of a smile at the corners of their mouths. If you go to the bank for a transaction, you might wait interminably for even the smallest request. But no one else seems to mind, and no one looks at the clock. Oh, the frustration we feel when our paperwork is processed with the speed of a glacier.

Despite such an accumulation of anecdotal evidence, skeptics will scorn my sentimentality. In fairness, I want to be honest. When abroad in more primitive conditions, I often miss modern conveniences—like a cold glass of milk or bathrooms without cockroaches. But what I don't miss are telephones, televisions, stoplights, video games, watches that beep during pastoral prayers, and boom boxes on the beach.

I have not gone so far as to suggest that the way of life in developing countries is superior or preferable to that of developed countries. I am only making the observation that these gracious and hospitable people are not exhausted, in body or spirit, whereas we often are. Those who would maintain that progress brings rest are wrong. We may have education, affluence, technology, leisure, and conveniences—but no rest.

God, however, has commanded us to rest. A biblically authentic and balanced life will include time to be still, to remember, to meditate, to delight in who He is and what He has made. But a large obstacle stands in our way: There is no glory in rest. No social acclaim. We are never a hero because we rest. We can only be still and better wait upon the Lord. We can only meditate upon the Word more. We can only have more margin with which to serve our neighbor. These things, however, are not socially reimbursable.

BURNING UP THE ENGINE

The healthiest lifestyle comes equipped with four gears.

The first gear is park for the contemplative times. This gear is used for rest and renewal, and to recharge our batteries. This is where we do much of our thinking about values and spirituality, as well as our study and prayer. It is the gear we use as we pick up a novel and head for the hammock, or as we sit on a stump and watch the wildlife.

The second gear is low. This gear is for relationships, for family and friends. This is the gear we use when talking with someone, and it prevents us from being distracted and nervously moving on to the next activity while still in the middle of a conversation. This is the gear we use when the children ask for a story or a back rub. Or when they ask about the death of pets, or sex, or God. No hurry here: just quality.

The third gear is drive. This is our usual gear for work and play. This gear uses lots of energy, and the faster speed feels good because it is productive. It gets us from place to place quickly. This is the gear we mow the lawn in or exercise in.

The fourth gear is overdrive. This gear is reserved for times that require extra effort. If we have a deadline coming, we kick into this gear. If we are playing a basketball game, we call upon overdrive to energize us. This is the gear doctors use during flu season when schedules are double-booked.

Unfortunately, many in our society do not shift down from overdrive. Our cars are not meant to race at high speeds continuously. Neither are our bodies or spirits. Yet to slow down for some is unthinkable and for others, impossible.

In our everyday lives, most of us need rest in three areas:

- Physical rest, the least important of the three.
- Emotional rest, more important by several orders of magnitude.
- Spiritual rest, which, though widely neglected, is of supreme importance.

PHYSICAL REST

Constant activity is a characteristic of our age. If we are not active, we feel slothful. If we are not productive, we feel guilty. A healthy twenty-eight-year-old man sitting on a lawn swing for an entire Sunday afternoon would likely feel the need to apologize to his neighbors should they discover him.

Such busyness does not come because our bodies can't help themselves. We cannot blame our thyroid or adrenal glands. Nor does it result from a theological teaching. It comes from a cultural value system that idolizes productivity. I am not saying that productivity is wrong. I am only saying it must not be idolized.

As a physician, I clearly affirm that physical activity is not only good, it is necessary. But so is physical rest. Our bodies were designed to need rest. Sleep is the clearest example, and one that cannot be violated. Many Americans, however, get the activity-rest cycle out of balance. Millions get too little activity, and millions more get too little rest. Type As, as an illustration, refuse to rest: to them it is an enemy. Also, those around them are made to feel weak if they desire a pause. Consequently, life is lived full speed ahead. They work hard, they play hard, and they even Sabbath hard.

Restless Work

Work in our culture often dominates other areas of life. To be sure, work is very important. But other activities are more important. The people who work the hardest and rest the least naturally rise to the top, from where they drive the entire work system. They set the rules, which maximize productivity. Even love and relationship come down the list. Little wonder rest cannot find a resting place.

"People in the Western world have leisure. We do not need to slave every minute in order to eat. But only a few appear to have rest," observes Mennonite author Doris Longacre. "Profit-making work began to swallow Sundays and holidays. Obviously much of this fatigue takes place in the name of making more money, even though the pantry's already stocked. After all, by burning a little more gas and working one more evening a week, it is possible to chase down one more account, open another store, or farm another field. But it may not be possible to love a spouse, children, and the friendless poor at the same time."[1]

God has instructed us that life is more than work. It includes relationships, worship, and yes, even rest. "A rest-less work style produces a rest-less person," notes Gordon MacDonald. "We do not rest because our work is done; we rest because God commanded it and created us to have a need for it."[2]

Lethal Leisure

Leisure might be the name we give our time away from work, but it is not a synonym for rest. Many can't understand why they are so tired after a vacation. The reason is because even our vacations and weekends have ceased to be restful.

Americans do not tolerate an activity vacuum well. The slow, contemplative life is largely foreign to our experience. Therefore, when "leisure time" appears on our schedule, we select from the many activity options society offers. This is not inherently wrong. Neither is quiet, introverted reflection always right. But when we work hard and then play harder, no wonder we feel fatigued so often.

Technology does not answer our need for physical rest. Laborsaving devices help in some respects, but curiously, those cultures that have the most laborsaving devices are the most hectic and the least rested. We often wonder why the homemaker remains so tired despite all the household appliances and conveniences. We forget to calculate that for every minute of time saved, our society offers hours of new activities, each with noise, expectations, and complexities of its own.

Although progress may not approve, *it is okay to rest physically*.

EMOTIONAL REST

More important to our overall health than physical rest is the resting of our emotions. Ask physicians about the frequency of anxiety or depression they find in their patients, and you will be stunned to learn how few in our midst are emotionally healthy and rested. We worry about our jobs, our marriages, our children, our looks, our age, our health, and our future. The high rate of tranquilizer use is an indicator of our lack of emotional rest.

Physical rest and emotional rest often go hand in hand, but we have no guarantee the resting of our bodies will produce rested psyches. The stilling of outward activity does not always assure a commensurate quieting of inward activity. Nevertheless, if we would rest our emotions, a wise first step would be to seek out quiet. Unfortunately, Walden is rarely found; lights and noise are to our right, people and action are to our left. With each successive decade, the ambient environmental noise level increases. Even within the four walls of home, televisions blare seven hours a day. Rock music has defrauded an entire adolescent generation out of anything even approximating emotional rest.

The majority of each day is spent with people. While that is exactly where we should be most of the time, it can be quite draining. For many, occasional solitude is a prerequisite for emotional resting, but where does one find privacy and silence?

Even the privilege of royalty doesn't always assure the privacy of rest. Near the end of his reign, England's King George V was asked what he would do if he could do whatever he pleased. "He replied that he would take his biggest car and drive and drive as far as it would take him. There he would find a little farmhouse, and in the farmhouse there would be a small, clean, whitewashed room, furnished only with a bed and an open fire. He would lie down on the bed, and lying so, alone in the small, clean room, he would look at the glowing coals of the fire, and the flames playing blue about them—and so he would rest. For once in a royal lifetime he would rest."[3]

Contemporary Commotion

If you think about it, you can find many reasons for the absence of emotional rest in our midst—so many, in fact, that it would be surprising to discover true restedness among us. Noise deprives us of rest, yet we have more noise today than ever before. Activity overload deprives us of rest, yet we are busier than ever. Inappropriate expectations deprive us of rest, yet our culture advertises: "You deserve the best." Pride deprives us of rest, as we worry about every wrinkle we have and every piece of clothing we wear. Discontent and covetousness deprive us of rest, yet our culturally sanctioned advertising intentionally stimulates discontent. "The proud man and the covetous man never have rest," noted Thomas à Kempis, "but the meek man and the poor in spirit live in great abundance of rest and peace."[4]

Preoccupation with success deprives us of rest—always climb a little higher and get a little more. So does preoccupation with power. Yet success and power are two cogs of the "American dream," and we are reluctant to let them go. Debt deprives us of rest, yet our debt is at unprecedented levels. We worry about our image and our reputation until we have no rest.

As A. W. Tozer observed, "The heart's fierce effort to protect itself from every slight, to shield its touchy honor from the bad opinion of friend and enemy, will never let the mind have rest."[5]

Restless Relationships

Perhaps the greatest root cause for the absence of emotional rest in our society is fractured relationships. When there is fighting in the workplace, contention in the community, bitterness in the church, and combat in the home, we won't find rest. The saddest of these, of course, is the home. It was intended by God as a haven of peace and security. But when strife enters, rest flees.

"If we don't deal with our unresolved conflicts, they'll deal with us," counsels Tim Kimmel. "Are there people whom you need to forgive? Do yourself a favor. Give them something they don't deserve but desperately need. Give them the gift of forgiveness. It's a gift that, once given, offers something in return. Your spirit gets a rest."[6]

If we would avoid the many unexpected pains of our day, we must discipline our expectations, tame our discontent, and mend our relationships.

For *it is important to rest emotionally*.

SPIRITUAL REST

When our bodies find rest, we feel refreshed. When our emotions find rest, our countenance is lifted. Yet relaxed muscles and minds are of little worth unless our souls also find rest in the acceptance of God. Such a rest transcends the problems of our world and shelters us where no injury can follow. As the psalmist writes, "He who dwells in the shelter of the Most High will rest in the shadow of the Almighty. I will say of the LORD, 'He is my refuge and my fortress, my God, in whom I trust.'"[7] The shadow of the Almighty is impregnable; His rest is ultimately the only dependable rest.

We should be concerned with at least two types of spiritual rest. God calls us to Sabbath rest. And He offers us surrendered rest.

Sabbath Rest

Someone once remarked, "God rested—and He wasn't tired." After creating, even the Almighty rested: "God blessed the seventh day and made it holy, because on it he rested from all the work of creating that he had done."[8] He looked on what He had made and delighted in it, and He has commanded us to do the same.

At Sabbath rest we don't simply rest the body—although that is important. Also, we don't primarily rest the emotions—although we would be wise to discover such rest in our Sabbaths. Instead, it is a remembrance. Moses writes, "Remember that you were slaves in Egypt and that the LORD your God brought you out of there with a mighty hand and an outstretched arm. Therefore the LORD your God has commanded you to observe the Sabbath day."[9] This same God who rescued the Israelites from their slavery in Egypt is the One who rescues us from our bondage to sin. Remember.

At Sabbath time we suspend dominion work and instead worship the dominion-Maker. We cease reaping for our own cupboards and instead bring an offering to Him. We rest not because we are tired. We don't cease our labor because it is finished. We don't worship because now there are grapes on the vine and cattle in the stalls. We rest and worship one day in seven simply because He is the Lord.

Remembering, worshiping, and resting are acts of contemplation. Yet churches today, for the most part, have not developed a practical theology of contemplation nor a practical theology of rest. The Sabbath rest is an opportunity for contemplation, an opportunity to remember our roots.

Surrendered Rest

"Softly and tenderly Jesus is calling"—but the world is shouting and waving its hands. Sometimes, over the din, it is hard to hear His invitation: "Ye who are weary come home." The Sabbath rest is a rest He *calls* us to, but the surrendered rest He *offers* to us. The Sabbath rest we enter out of obedience; the surrendered rest we enter out of our need. The Sabbath rest arises from the good and perfect law of God; the surrendered rest arises from the good and perfect grace of God. The Sabbath rest is remembrance; the surrendered rest is meekness. Both provide soothing, God-ordained healing.

High on my list of favorite Scriptures are Jesus' words in Matthew 11:28-30: "Come to me, all you who are weary and burdened, and I will give you rest. Take my yoke upon you and learn from me, for I am gentle and humble in heart, and you will find rest for your souls. For my yoke is easy and my burden is light." These words draw weary people everywhere. Yet, per usual, Jesus leaves us scratching our heads. What does He mean, to take His yoke? I'm not sure that sounds restful. It sounds more like suffering.

MEEKNESS

The answer lies in meekness. In this passage, Christ calls Himself "gentle and humble"—meek. He came not to judge but to die. He came not to shout and defend the honor of the Father but to die. He came not to fight but to die. No persecution could disturb Him for He came to suffer. Yet all the time He was suffering, He knew He was winning.

We, too, can suffer and win. We can live with love even when others hate—all the time knowing that love wins. We can respond with grace when others fight, knowing that grace wins. When we come to Him and surrender, accepting His yoke, we accept full vulnerability to the onslaught of the world. Yet, at the same time, we are assured that nothing can separate us from the victorious love of Christ. This rest is a self-weakening unto God-strength. It is a self-emptying unto God-fullness. It is the rest of full surrender.

Teaches A. W. Tozer:

> Jesus calls us to His rest, and meekness is His method. The meek man cares not at all who is greater than he, for he has long ago decided that the esteem of the world is not worth the effort. The rest Christ offers is the rest of meekness, the blessed relief which

comes when we accept ourselves for what we are and cease to pretend. It will take some courage at first, but the needed grace will come as we learn that we are sharing this new and easy yoke with the strong Son of God Himself.[10]

In an age of strife and unrest, when our bodies are weary and our spirits are frenzied, "Don't worry, be happy," will not rescue us. I prefer Corrie ten Boom's "Don't wrestle, just nestle." Even when I feel inferior, even when I have been victimized, even when the pace and pressures of life bring me to the point of collapse, Christ brings me to His rest. When my surrender is completed and His yoke is accepted, then my soul will find rest. And *it is imperative, in such an age as ours, that we rest spiritually.*

PAIN, MARGIN, HEALTH, AND RELATIONSHIP

> History is something that happens to people; what happens is always different from what people would rather have done....We have made great progress—for which we also have paid a price.[1]
>
> —Claude Lévi-Strauss,
> French anthropologist

HUMANS ARE PASSIVE agents. It is true that, from time to time, we make small and even a few large changes attempting to improve matters. But mostly our lives are filled with passivity.

At this juncture, however, allowing history to just "happen to us" is unforgivably foolish. For no matter what their ideological bent, the trend watchers are united in one opinion: Something is afoot. Along with much of the rest of the world, the United States is in a period of profound disequilibrium. Having never been through a disjuncture of such dimension or consisting of such particulars before, we are not quite sure in what condition we will find ourselves when it leaves off.

In this unfolding of historic change, we have been guided by the process of history called progress. In many respects, progress has done a good job, bringing us places previously reserved for fantasy writers. And at such speed! But progress has been painful of late.

WHAT TO DO WITH PAIN

At times it appears as if the cumulative weight of suffering and sorrow will sink the entire world. People hurt, families hurt, friendships hurt, churches hurt, communities hurt, nations hurt. What should we do about all this pain?

First, let's thank God for it. Anything that redirects us to Him is of benefit.

Second, let's repent. Not the "ineffectual, unfervent prayer of an unrighteous man availeth little" kind of repentance, but the kind that means something and costs something. The kind of repentance where you conduct business with God; and thereafter, life has actually changed and you are headed in a different direction.

Third, let's do some surgery. There is a lot of pruning that needs to be done and abscesses that need draining. Let's prune away the time cancers, amputate the energy tumors, and drain the debt abscesses. Don't cringe— God is a great physician, and it is good to be pruned and drained. We ought to do it more often. For without surgery, margin and health will not return.

Fourth, let's cooperate with God. Our hope for the future is only valid because of one fact: God is still around, and what's more, He's still interested. Our success or failure will hinge on our cooperation with Him. "When this little life is over," wrote J. B. Phillips, "nearly all that makes the headlines in the newspapers or fills the bulletins on the radio will seem to be of purely temporary significance. But the work of those who have cooperated with God will remain, for it is part of his everlasting purpose."[2]

SHORT TERM, LONG TERM

When we contact God to tell Him we are ready to cooperate, He will give us a two-term plan: short and long.

For the short term, we need worry only about today. Isn't that good news? Isn't that hopeful? Plan for tomorrow, to be sure. Be concerned for tomorrow. But worry only about today.[3]

You see, our responsibility is to do what is right today. Of course the future is important; of course we are concerned about what kind of society we end up with; of course we must plan intelligently and prayerfully. But we can only get there one day at a time, and today is the day to do what is right.

Today we must begin valuing the things God values and cease valuing those things of no value to Him. Today we must agree that our choices do make a difference—whether we live without margin, work two jobs, build an expensive house, overload a friend, don't spend time with our children. Today let's decide to invest in relationship, to encourage someone. Today decide to love, the sacrificial-service kind of love. Today forgive someone who should have been forgiven long ago. Today light one little candle and stop cursing the darkness.

For the long term, God would have us set about rebuilding using the instructions previously given. He has already told us what to do—now we just have to do it.

Let me tell you another hopeful secret about God's plan. He wants us to reclaim society, but not necessarily as the first order of business. Redeeming what we can of progress will be a huge job, but we can work on that tomorrow. For now, we have enough work at home to keep us occupied. So put away the newspaper, turn off the nightly news, and forget about the despair of problem mountain. We will return to them later. It is time to put on the work clothes and report for duty in the front yard.

Here God awaits us, with the confidence of a Leader who has been through it all before. As we become teachable—even desperate—what will be His advice? He has, of course, already given us lots of instructions. But if we were to boil them all out, one principle would rise to the top: the priority of relationship.

GOD'S REPORT CARD

If God's greatest commandments are as inclusive as I believe they are, when life is over and we receive our report card, it will have only one category—relationship. There will be three lines:

- How did we relate to God?
- How did we relate to ourselves?
- How did we relate to others?

We know that relationship is so important to God because He does all His work there. That is why progress missed Him. Progress kept telling us to search for buried treasure inside bank vaults, while all the time God had it buried in the heart of our neighbor.

Even if we have little time for healthy relationships, we all instinctually understand their importance. Due to the antagonistic influences of marginless living, however, they are an increasingly rare commodity. Overloaded contemporary life attempts to de-relationalize us, which is perhaps the English equivalent of the German word *Zerrissenheit*—"torn-to-pieces-hood." Today, it is possible to live in a city surrounded by one million people and be alone for a lifetime. We become a number, and no one ever loved a number. The systems of modernity swallow us alive. Bureaucracies, corporations, institutions—all conjure up images of structures that inhale people and exhale cement.

God, however, is a personal God, and relationship is important to Him. He created us as relational beings—not because He had to but because it suited Him. We are relational and dependent whether we acknowledge it or not, whether we want to be or not. We ought not kick against this, however, for it was meant as a gift. God gave us to each other for reasons of benefit, not torture.

RELATE TO WHOM?

How do we know that God's report card contains three categories? Jesus told us so. When asked outright by the Pharisee, Jesus answered that, of course, the *Shema* was the greatest commandment: "'Hear, O Israel, the Lord our God, the Lord is one. Love the Lord your God with all your heart and with all your soul and with all your mind and with all your strength.'" However, He did not stop there: "The second is this: 'Love your neighbor as yourself.' There is no commandment greater than these."[4]

In so answering, Christ laid out for us the greatest imperative of eternity: to love God, our neighbor, and our self. This commandment must be the first guideline for all of life's decisions and actions. Nothing is to come before it.

Love the Lord your God. God is our Creator, which means we were related to Him even before birth. He yearns for our broken relationship to be reconciled. He went 99.99 percent of the way and extends a nail-pierced hand for us to grasp. His patience has given us much space to repent. We live in a world that promotes distance, builds fences, buys locks, and doesn't talk on elevators. But God, in Christ, says, "Come."

Love yourself. God assumes we love and care for self. Some people, however, have no relationship with themselves. To leave them alone in solitude for a day would be punishment. That we are worthy of love is demonstrated by the fact that God loves us. His love validates our worth and, as a matter of fact, provides the only basis for it. Without that validation we stand undeserving. Some are so broken by this unworthiness that they get stuck in it. The concept of unworthiness is a wonderful thing to grasp and is the first step in setting things right. But getting stuck in it is a spiritually neurotic thing to do and is not God's will. The call to spiritually accurate self-love is not a denial of our unworthiness but is instead the result of a journey that goes through unworthiness to God.

Love your neighbor. Created incapable of meeting all our own needs, God gave us others, in relationship, to help. Despite the fact that each individual is of more value than all the careers, education, and money in the universe added together and multiplied times infinity, rightly relating to others seems to be the most difficult item on the contemporary agenda.

QUIET KINDNESSES

God has shown us the road to health, the path to blessing—it is the way of relationship. Do you see now why careers, degrees, and estates can never quite get the job done? Somehow we just keep taking our expensive automobiles to our posh offices to make another hundred thousand dollars, while all the time our relationships vaporize before our eyes and our loneliness deepens.

But we are not helpless. Progress does not own us. We do not have to let history "happen to us." We are free to change. And God is still interested in lending a hand.

We can focus on relationship and create a margin for it. We can simplify and balance our lives so that relationships have some space. We can invest ourselves in other people. When we don't feel like it, we can still do it. Even when we can't find anyone else interested in friendship, we can always start spreading around quiet kindnesses, expecting none in return.

Soon, love will begin to flow out from us, and with the flow there will also come a flowing back. For love, you see, is "the most excellent way."[5]

LOVE

All the commandments in Scripture reduce to Christ's Great Commandment, and the Great Commandment reduces to one concept: love.

God is in love with His creation. The creature has something of the Creator in him, and God has loved us from the beginning. Even when the creature turned his back on heaven, yet God loved him: "I made you, and I will carry you. I don't hold anything against you. Let me rescue you."

The history of the world reduces to this: your being pursued by love. He courted you; He followed you; He loved you. If you go to work or school or church, He is there. If you go to the edge of the universe or to the borders of hell, He is there. If you go deep inside yourself, He is there. In the dark of the night, in your depression, He is there. On your deathbed, when you don't want anybody to leave you, He is there. If you look behind you or before you, He is there, waiting to be allowed entrance into your life.

In the economics of eternity, God paid a great price. If we only better understood the cost, we would also better understand our worth.

THE ECONOMICS OF THE RELATIONAL LIFE

Love is the currency of the relational life. In the relational life, we spend love and receive love. That was God's idea from the beginning. It is what He taught us, and it was what He showed us. God wants us to spend love freely, even generously. When we do, everyone becomes rich. It is the primary currency of God's economics.

As you can see, love is not like other resources. There is an infinite supply. You can use it and use it and use it. Yet there will still be more left over. As a matter of fact, *the more it is used, the more its supply increases.*

Some guard their supply of love, doling it out in portions. But this kind of thinking works with money, not with love. With money, the more you hoard, the richer you become. But *with love, the more you spend, the richer you become.*

Spending and receiving love is the best part of kingdom work. It is also the best part of doctoring.

FLOWERS FROM THE OTHER SIDE OF THE GRAVE

Eileen was sixty-three years old and already had advanced cancer when I first met her. Following surgery, there was little that could be done.

She healed nicely from her operation but, some months later, developed a persistent cough. "It is probably the tumor, Eileen," I said. "We should get a chest X-ray to be sure."

"No, doctor," she replied. "I don't want to know anything about it." Soon, however, her shortness of breath left us no choice but to investigate.

"It's as we suspected," I said. "Your X-ray shows a large amount of fluid in the right lung. If you would like, we can make you more comfortable by draining some of the fluid off here in the office. It really doesn't hurt much, and you should be able to breathe easier."

Under normal circumstances, tapping the lung is always followed by an X-ray to make sure the lung has not been punctured or deflated during the procedure. But after three uneventful taps in the clinic, I decided to deviate from protocol and do the procedure in Eileen's home. By now, she was having great difficulty getting around.

Each time I went to her home, I would first sit on the bed and we would talk. Then I would examine her lungs, position her for the procedure, and introduce the needle into her chest.

On the third visit, I held her hand for a while, and together we looked out the open window. Perhaps we both sensed the end was near.

"Those are beautiful lilacs," I said, noticing for the first time the flowers hardly a foot or two outside her open window. They were just coming into full bloom, and the room was full of their fragrance.

"Lilacs are my favorite," she replied. "That is why I wanted to be down here, close to them. I love them."

After draining another quart of fluid off her lung, I left the house for the last time. A week later she died.

Shortly after Eileen's death, her daughter came to the clinic carrying a huge bouquet of deep purple lilacs in a blue mason jar. She asked the receptionist to bring the flowers to my office, explaining that it would be too hard for her to see me just then.

This note was with the lilacs:

> Words do seem inadequate to express our thanks for all you have done for our family. Because of your kind, caring ways Mom was able to stay in her home and be as comfortable as possible.
>
> Mom wanted the "Best Doctor in the World" to enjoy her special lilacs. God bless you!

I have received many expressions of thanks from the relatives of deceased patients. But this was the first time I had been given flowers from the other side of the grave.

I am not the "Best Doctor in the World." But at least for a moment, I felt like it. Medicine can be a grinding profession when money is the only reward. But when love is the currency of exchange, gratitude alone can pay the debt in full.

Must We Love?

I did not drain the fluid off Eileen's lung because I am a technician who enjoys doing procedures. I did not visit her in the home because I am a businessman looking for increased revenue. Instead, I cared for her because I allowed her ache to enter my heart.

Eileen was suffering, and I had the skills to help. I reached out to her, not as a proceduralist or a profiteer, but as a physician. My reaching is what I call love. Why should I work just for money when I can work for love? And from the other side of the grave, Eileen reached back. I call that love too. Relational economics.

Somehow, we just can't wrap our minds around this idea of love. We can't nail it down and say, "There, I've got you." Yes, love is strange. It is weak yet tough, vulnerable yet strong. It chooses to lose but can never be beaten. It puts itself last yet always leads the way. It is mysterious, yet it came in flesh and stood before us. It is death—yet it is life.

God's love is commonly undervalued and always underestimated. No virtue can compete with it, and no vice can defeat it. God ordained that it should be so, and He stands guard to see that no one changes the order of things.

Must we love? That is a nonsensical question. It is like asking, "Must we breathe?" No, we do not have to breathe, and no, we do not have to love. But the consequences of both those decisions will be the same.

Are You Ready?

Pain surrounds us all. Much of this pain comes from progress's blatant disregard for our need of margin. And much of this pain—far too much of this pain—is because of neglected and broken relationships. It is difficult to be healthy in a society where relational, emotional, and spiritual sickness is endemic. If you live in a swamp, malaria has a head start.

But do you know what? Malaria can be treated, and so can pain. Margin can be restored. Broken relationships can be healed. It takes work.

It takes love. It might even take going to the cross. But healing is worth it. I have never seen a truly healthy person who didn't derive that well-being from the benefits of intact, loving relationships.

Are you ready to commit to relationship in love? This is not like asking, "Would you go to the store for some milk?" but more like, "Are you ready to lay down your life for your friends?"[6]

If you are, then do everything you can to travel in the health direction. If stress crushes your spirit by poisoning you with despair, then either conquer stress or walk away—but don't stop relating. If overload destroys your relationships, then dispatch overload to the far side. If that malignant, universal enemy of relational health, marginless living, leaves you panting for air and desperate for space, then go and take margin back. Hack it out of your cultural landscape. And guard it for the sake of your God, yourself, your family, and your friends.

Health cannot be far behind.

APPENDIX

Graphs Demonstrating Exponential Change

THESE GRAPHS VISUALLY demonstrate the rapid and unprecedented changes within American society. It is important to note the slope of the curves. Curves that slope rapidly upward in this way are called exponential. Some of the graphs appearing here are true exponential slopes, while others only approximate exponential slopes for a period of time. The point is, all these graphs illustrate rapid, radical change.

Most of these graphs have a standardized time frame, from 1900 to 2000. A few, however, go back two thousand years.

The reason margin disappeared as quickly as it did is because of the type of exponential slopes found on these graphs. Remember straight line graphs represent historical transition; exponential curve graphs represent historical disruption.

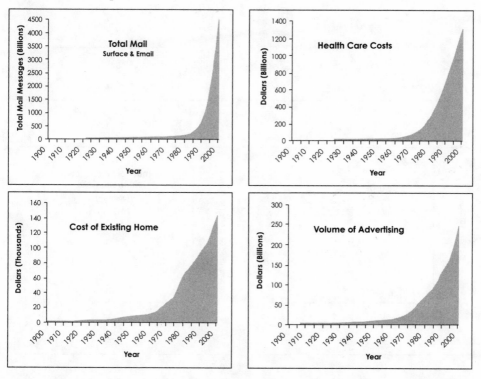

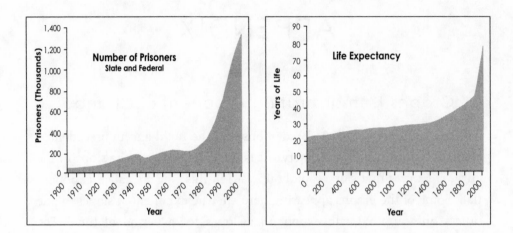

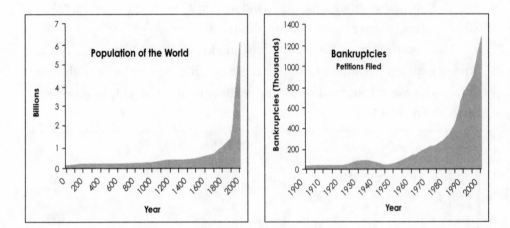

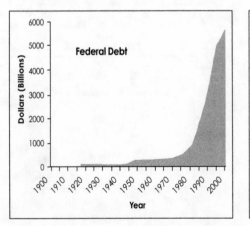

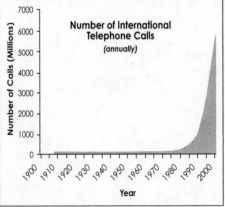

NOTES

CHAPTER 2—THE PAIN OF PROGRESS

1. Robert Nisbet, *History of the Idea of Progress* (New York: Basic Books, 1980), pp. 4-5, 7.

2. Nicholas Wolterstorff, *Until Justice and Peace Embrace* (Grand Rapids: Eerdmans, 1983), pp. 25, 64.

3. Richard A. Swenson, M.D., *The Overload Syndrome: Learning to Live Within Your Limits* (Colorado Springs: NavPress, 1998), pp. 39-48.

4. E. F. Schumacher, *Small Is Beautiful: Economics as if People Mattered* (New York: Harper & Row, 1973), p. 157.

5. William Wilberforce, *Real Christianity: Contrasted with the Prevailing Religious System* (Portland, OR: Multnomah, 1982 first published 1829), p. 91.

6. "This is what the LORD says: 'Let not the wise man boast of his wisdom or the strong man boast of his strength or the rich man boast of his riches, but let him who boasts boast about this: that he understands and knows me, that I am the LORD, who exercises kindness, justice and righteousness on earth, for in these I delight,' declares the LORD" (Jeremiah 9:23-24).

7. Wilberforce, p. 123.

CHAPTER 3—THE PAIN OF PROBLEMS

1. Mark A. Noll, George M. Marsden, and Nathan O. Hatch, *The Search for Christian America* (Colorado Springs: Helmers and Howard, 1989), pp. 148, 152.

CHAPTER 4—THE PAIN OF STRESS

1. Hans Selye, M.D., *Stress Without Distress* (New York: New American Library, 1974), p. 14.
2. E. F. Schumacher, *Good Work* (New York: Harper & Row, 1979), p. 25.
3. Nadya Labi, "Burning Out at Nine?" *Time*, 23 November 1998, p. 86.
4. Susan H. Greenberg and Karen Springen, "The Overscheduled Baby," *Newsweek* Special Issue, October 2000, p. 79.

CHAPTER 5—THE PAIN OF OVERLOAD

1. Alvin Toffler, *Future Shock* (New York: Bantam, 1970), pp. 351-352.
2. Richard J. Foster, *Freedom of Simplicity* (New York: Harper & Row, 1981), p. 91.
3. Philippians 4:13, NKJV.
4. Robert Banks, *The Tyranny of Time: When 24 Hours Is Not Enough* (Downers Grove, IL: InterVarsity, 1983), p. 45.
5. Arthur M. Schlesinger, Jr., "The Modern Consciousness and the Winged Chariot," *The Personal Experience of Time,* eds. S. Gorman and A. E. Wessmann (New York: Plenum, 1977), p. 269.
6. Barry Schwartz, *The Paradox of Choice: Why More Is Less* (New York: HarperCollins, 2004), p. 2.
7. J. Grant Howard, *Balancing Life's Demands: A New Perspective on Priorities* (Portland, OR: Multnomah, 1983), p. 144.

CHAPTER 6—MARGIN

1. Mildred Tengbom, "Harried Lives: If You're a Frenzied Mess, It's Time to Decide What's Really Important to You," *Focus on the Family,* October 1985, pp. 11-12.
2. Robert F. Greene, M.D., "True Confession: I Enjoyed My Year Abroad as a Short-Term Missionary," *Christian Medical and Dental Society Journal,* Winter 1990, p. 17.

CHAPTER 7—MARGIN IN EMOTIONAL ENERGY

1. Louis H. Evans, Jr., *Covenant to Care* (Wheaton, IL: Victor, 1977), pp. 80-81.

2. ". . . the burden of psychiatric conditions has been heavily underestimated . . ." *National Institute of Health (NIH) Publication* No. 01-4586, 1 January 2001, *http://www.nimh.nih.gov/publicat/burden.cfm*

3. Tom Sine, *The Mustard Seed Conspiracy* (Waco, TX: Word, 1981), p. 81.

4. Jack Dreyfus, *A Remarkable Medicine Has Been Overlooked* (New York: Simon and Schuster, 1970), pp. 26-27.

5. Gregg Easterbrook, *The Progress Paradox: How Life Gets Better While People Feel Worse* (New York: Random House, 2003), pp. 163-165.

6. Frederic Flach, M.D., *Resilience: Discovering a New Strength at Times of Stress* (New York: Fawcett Columbine, 1988), p. 35.

7. Mark 6:30-32.

8. "The Biology of Laughter," quoting Lee Berk, *The Futurist*, March-April 2002, p. 2.

9. John Townsend, *Hiding from Love: How to Change the Withdrawal Patterns That Isolate and Imprison You* (Colorado Springs: NavPress, 1991), pp. 80-82.

10. Quoted by Arthur F. Holmes, *Contours of a World View* (Grand Rapids: Eerdmans, 1983), p. 12.

11. Thomas à Kempis, *The Imitation of Christ,* trans. Richard Whitford (New York: Washington Square Press, 1953 [1424]), p. 3.

12. 1 Corinthians 13:13, emphasis added.

13. Flach, p. 259.

14. Armand Mayo Nicholi II, "Why Can't I Deal with Depression?" *Christianity Today*, 11 November 1983, p. 40.

15. Nicholi, pp. 40-41.

16. Diogenes Allen, *Christian Belief in a Postmodern World: The Full Wealth of Conviction* (Louisville, KY: Westminster/John Knox, 1989), pp. 5, 126.

17. Romans 5:2-5.

18. Colossians 3:14.

19. Hans Selye, M.D., *Stress Without Distress* (New York: New American Library, 1974), p. 124.

20. 1 Corinthians 13:13, emphasis added.

CHAPTER 8—MARGIN IN PHYSICAL ENERGY

1. Psalm 127:2.
2. Kenneth H. Cooper, M.D., *Aerobics* (New York: Bantam, 1968),
   pp. 62, 107.

CHAPTER 9—MARGIN IN TIME

1. Quoted by Daniel J. Boorstin, *The Discoverers* (New York: Random
   House, 1983), p. 25.
2. Boorstin, p. 39.
3. Benjamin Hunnicutt, "When We Had the Time," *Take Back Your
   Time*, ed. John de Graaf (San Francisco: Berrett-Koehler Publishers,
   Inc., 2003), p. 117.
4. Nancy Gibbs, "How America Has Run Out of Time," *Time*, 24 April
   1989, p. 59.
5. Juliet Schor, "The (Even More) Overworked American," *Take Back
   Your Time*, ed. John de Graaf (San Francisco: Berrett-Koehler
   Publishers, Inc., 2003), p. 7.
6. "New International Labor Organization (ILO) Study shows U.S.
   Workers Put in Longest Hours," *http://kilm.ilo.org/press* Package
   2001, asp, 2 September 2001.
7. "The Changing Organization of Work and the Safety and Health of
   Working People," *Center for Disease Control and Prevention and
   National Institute for Occupational Safety and Health*, 9 May 2002,
   page 1, *http://www.cdc.gov/niosh/pdfs/02-116.pdf*
8. Peggy Noonan, "There Is No Time, There Will Be Time," WSJ.com
   Opinion Journal from *The Wall Street Journal* Editorial Page, 18
   September 2001,
   http://www.opinionjournal.com/forms/printThis.html?id=95001157
9. E. F. Schumacher, *Good Work* (New York: Harper & Row, 1979),
   p. 25.
10. Robert J. Samuelson, "Fun Ethic vs. Work Ethic?" *Newsweek*, 10
    September 2001, p. 43.
11. Quoted in Robert Banks, *The Tyranny of Time: When 24 Hours Is Not
    Enough* (Downers Grove, IL: InterVarsity, 1983), p. 66.

12. Quoted in Gibbs, p. 61.

13. James Dobson, *Dr. Dobson Answers Your Questions* (Wheaton, IL: Tyndale, 1982), pp. 27-28.

14. Nancy Ann Jeffrey, "Whatever Happened to Friendship?" *The Wall Street Journal*, 3 March 2000, p. W1.

15. Steven Levy, "Hello Again," *Newsweek*, 18 May 1998, p. 47.

16. "Wisdom for Ministry," compiled by Richard A. Kauffman, *Christianity Today*, November 2003, p. 75.

17. Nathan Bierma, "Bad Habits of the High-Tech Heart," *Books & Culture*, November/December 2002, p. 30.

18. Jean Fleming, *Between Walden and the Whirlwind: Living the Christ-Centered Life* (Colorado Springs: NavPress, 1985), p. 40.

19. Gordon MacDonald, *Restoring Your Spiritual Passion* (Nashville: Oliver-Nelson, 1986), pp. 24-25.

20. Fleming, p. 43.

21. Rick Warren, "Quote," *Current Thoughts & Trends*, August 2003, p. 24.

22. Nancy Yanes Hoffman, "Meyer Friedman: Type A Behavior Cardiovascular Research Continues," *The Journal of the American Medical Association*, 252, 21 September 1984, pp. 1392-1393.

23. Bruce Larson, *There's a Lot More to Health Than Not Being Sick* (Waco, TX: Word, 1981), p. 114.

24. Dietrich Bonhoeffer, *Life Together* (New York: Harper and Brothers, 1954), p. 99.

CHAPTER 10—MARGIN IN FINANCES

1. Norman Mailer, Interviewed, "Something Has Been Stolen from Us That We Can't Name," *U.S. News and World Report*, 23 May 1983, pp. 73-74.

2. Romans 13:8.

3. Larry Burkett, *Major Purchases* (Chicago: Moody, 1991), p. 19.

4. Proverbs 22:7.

5. Romans 6:18-19, 1 Corinthians 7:23, Galatians 5:13.

6. Doris Janzen Longacre, *Living More with Less* (Scottdale, PA: Herald, 1980), p. 97.

7. Matthew 6:19-21.

8. 1 Timothy 6:9-11.

9. 1 John 3:17.

10. Additional verses that speak to this issue are found in Proverbs 3:27-28: "Do not withhold good from those who deserve it, when it is in your power to act. Do not say to your neighbor, 'Come back later; I'll give it tomorrow'—when you now have it with you."

11. Gregg Easterbrook, *The Progress Paradox: How Life Gets Better While People Feel Worse* (New York: Random House, 2003), p. 177.

12. Jacques Ellul, *Money and Power,* trans. LaVonne Neff (Downers Grove, IL: InterVarsity, 1984), p. 88.

13. Ellul, p. 110.

14. E. F. Schumacher, *Small Is Beautiful: Economics as if People Mattered* (New York: Harper & Row, 1973), p. 33.

15. Matthew 6:33, NKJV.

CHAPTER 11—HEALTH THROUGH CONTENTMENT

1. 1 Timothy 6:6, Hebrews 13:5.

2. Philippians 4:12.

3. J. I. Packer, "The Secret of Contentment," Address given at Wheaton College, Wheaton, Illinois, 27 February 1984.

4. 1 Corinthians 4:9-13.

5. 2 Corinthians 11:23-27.

6. Philippians 4:11-12.

7. A. W. Tozer, *The Pursuit of God* (Harrisburg, PA: Christian Publications, 1948), p. 20.

8. Nguyen Thi An, "A Letter Written to a Vietnamese Friend in Canada," *Alliance Life,* 10 December 1986, p. 17. Used by permission.

9. 1 Timothy 6:8.

10. John Kenneth Galbraith, *The Affluent Society* (New York: Mentor Books, 1958), p. 128.

11. Packer, "The Secret of Contentment."

12. Herbert Schlossberg, *Idols for Destruction: Christian Faith and Its Confrontation with American Society* (Nashville: Nelson, 1983), p. 136.

13. John White, *The Golden Cow: Materialism in the Twentieth-Century Church* (Downers Grove, IL: InterVarsity, 1979), p. 61.

14. Quoted by L. S. Stavrianos, *The Promise of the Coming Dark Age* (San Francisco: W. H. Freeman and Company, 1976), p. 165.

15. Hebrews 13:5.

16. Tozer, p. 22.

17. Doug Trouten, "Discontent Is the New Spirit of the Age," *Twin Cities Christian,* 13 September 1984, p. 6.

18. Joseph Katz, ed., *The Poems of Stephen Crane* (New York: Cooper Square Publishers, 1966), p. 102. Originally published in Stephen Crane's book of poetry entitled *War Is Kind,* 1899.

19. Packer, "The Secret of Contentment."

20. Thomas Watson, *The Art of Divine Contentment* (Glasgow, Scotland: Free Presbyterian Publications, reprint of 1855 edition), pp. 16, 22.

21. Jeremiah Burroughs, *The Rare Jewel of Christian Contentment* (Edinburgh, Scotland: The Banner of Truth Trust, 1987 [1648]), p. 19.

CHAPTER 12—HEALTH THROUGH SIMIPLICITY

1. John Charles Cooper, *The Joy of the Plain Life* (Nashville: Benson, 1981), p. 106.

2. John 13:15-16.

3. "To this you were called, because Christ suffered for you, leaving you an example, that you should follow in his steps" (1 Peter 2:21).

4. "Your attitude should be the same as that of Christ Jesus" (Philippians 2:5). "But made himself nothing, taking the very nature of a servant, being made in human likeness" (verse 7).

5. Tom Allen, "Living Like the King," *Alliance Life,* 10 June 1981, pp. 5-6.

6. David E. Shi, *The Simple Life: Plain Living and High Thinking in American Culture* (New York: Oxford University Press, 1985), p. 3.

7. Arthur G. Gish, *Beyond the Rat Race* (New Canaan, CT: Keats Publishing, 1973), pp. 73-74.

8. Quoted by Shi, p. 200.

9. "He has showed you, O man, what is good. And what does the LORD require of you? To act justly and to love mercy and to walk humbly with your God" (Micah 6:8).

CHAPTER 13—HEALTH THROUGH BALANCE
1. David M. Baughan, M.D., "Contemporary Scientific Principles and Family Medicine," *Family Medicine,* 19, January/February 1987, p. 42.
2. Richard H. Bube, "On the Pursuit of Excellence: Pitfalls in the Effort to Become No. 1," *Perspectives on Science and Christian Faith,* June 1987, pp. 70-71. Used by permission.
3. J. Grant Howard, *Balancing Life's Demands: A New Perspective on Priorities* (Portland, OR: Multnomah, 1994), p. 38.
4. George Rust, M.D., "The Balancing Act," *Christian Medical Society Journal,* Winter 1983, p. 8.
5. Anne Morrow Lindbergh, *Gift from the Sea* (New York: Pantheon, 1955), p. 120.

CHAPTER 14—HEALTH THROUGH REST
1. Doris Janzen Longacre, *Living More with Less* (Scottdale, PA: Herald, 1980), pp. 210-211.
2. Gordon MacDonald, *Ordering Your Private World* (Nashville: Oliver-Nelson, 1984), pp. 166, 174.
3. Marjorie Barstow Greenbie, *In Quest of Contentment* (New York: McGraw-Hill, 1936), p. 57.
4. Thomas à Kempis, *The Imitation of Christ,* trans. Richard Whitford (New York: Washington Square Press, 1953 [1424]), p. 13.
5. A. W. Tozer, *The Pursuit of God* (Harrisburg, PA: Christian Publications, 1948), p. 112.
6. Tim Kimmel, *Little House on the Freeway: Help for the Hurried Home* (Portland, OR: Multnomah, 1987), pp. 63, 66.
7. Psalm 91:1-2.
8. Genesis 2:3.
9. Deuteronomy 5:15.
10. Tozer, pp. 112, 116.

CHAPTER 15—PAIN, MARGIN, HEALTH, AND RELATIONSHIP

1. Claude Lévi-Strauss, as quoted by Linda Rogers, "'Passive' Progress," *World Press Review*, December 1983, p. 41.
2. J. B. Phillips, *For This Day*, ed. Denis Duncan (Waco, TX: Word, 1974), p. 180.
3. "Therefore do not worry about tomorrow, for tomorrow will worry about itself. Each day has enough trouble of its own" (Matthew 6:34).
4. Mark 12:29-31.
5. "Now I will show you the most excellent way" (1 Corinthians 12:31).
6. See John 15:13.

INDEX

AUTHOR

RICHARD A. SWENSON, M.D., is a physician, researcher, futurist, author, and educator. He received his B.S. in physics Phi Beta Kappa from Denison University and his M.D. from the University of Illinois School of Medicine. Following five years of private practice and fifteen years of clinical teaching with the University of Wisconsin Medical School, he currently conducts research and writes full time about the future of the world system, culture, faith, and healthcare.

Dr. Swenson has traveled to over fifty countries with a year of study in Europe and medical work in developing countries. He is the author of six books, including *Margin, The Overload Syndrome, More Than Meets The Eye,* and *A Minute Of Margin.* His presentations include a wide variety of career, professional, educational, medical and management groups, most major church denominations, Congress, and the Pentagon. He was an invited guest participant for the 44th Annual National Security Seminar and is a recent recipient of Christian Medical Association's Educator of the Year Award.

Dr. Swenson and his wife, Linda, live in Menomonie, Wisconsin. They have two sons, Matthew and Adam, and a daughter-in-law Maureen.